Ghosts of London

The East End, City and North

by J. A. Brooks

Jarrold Colour Publications, Norwich

0 7117 0039 7
© Copyright 1982 Jarrold and Sons Ltd, Norwich, England.
Printed and published in Great Britain by Jarrold and Sons Ltd, Norwich. 182

Introduction

'How common these dead, nameless, unreckt things grow.'

Soon after starting work on *Ghosts of London* it became obvious that such a wealth of material could hardly be contained in two small volumes, let alone one. Thus the work is divided on arbitrary geographical lines: this part deals with the City and East End plus the northern and eastern suburbs. The second volume takes in the remainder, with an emphasis on supernatural activity in the West End.

Both books contain a few episodes that would seem to have little to do with any sort of ghost, but since they pleased my ghoulish sense of humour I included them. I apologise to all those who do not share my delight in the misfortunes of those such as the beadle of the Royal College of Surgeons who died of shock after seeing a corpse appear to come to life during an early experiment with electricity.

Choosing the illustrations has been a particularly enjoyable task, and I am grateful to all those who have helped me in this, most notably Ralph Hyde of the Guildhall Library.

The Society for Psychical Research has been generous in allowing me to use their material on the Bethnal Green Ghost, and I would also like to thank Mr P. J. L. Rose, the son of one of those involved in the case, for correcting the first draft of that chapter.

The cover photograph shows 'Old Jimmy' Garlickhythe, whose semi-fossilised remains are kept in a case at St James's, Garlickhythe, one of the City churches rebuilt by Wren. 'Old Jimmy' died in medieval times: his body survived the Fire of London (when St James's was burnt down) and it is said to walk occasionally in the nave of the church to the terror of unwary visitors.

Contents

The East End

Bow is at the heart of the Cockney's London, for only those born within hearing of its church bells can truly be called Cockney. The ghosts of Bow are wise in their choice of haunts – nearly all of them are pubs.

Most famous of these is the Bow Bells – an article in the *East London Advertiser* in 1974 spoke of the 'phantom flusher' that made going to the loo a nightmare for ladies at the pub. Customers seated on the toilet would be startled by the locked door being thrown open, and the cistern emptied by an unseen hand. The landlord once felt an icy wind when all the doors were closed, and saw an inexplicable mist rise from the floor. When a seance was held to solve the mystery the toilet door crashed open, shattering the glass of its windows.

Another Bow Road pub with a ghost is the Black Swan. On the night of 23 September 1916, the original pub was completely destroyed by a bomb dropped by a Zeppelin in one of the first aerial attacks on London. Four people were killed – the landlord's two young daughters (aged twenty and twenty-one), the baby girl of the elder daughter, and his mother. The pub was subsequently rebuilt, but the ghosts of Cissie and Sylvia Reynolds, the two pretty daughters, remain and have been seen in several of the rooms, particularly the cellar, where there have been many strange incidents. Beer taps have seemingly turned themselves off, and barrels which were lifted on to the racks full have been found empty the next day, without having a pint pulled from them. On one occasion beer taps were turned on in the middle of the night in the bar, causing a flood of bitter. The German Shepherd dog kept by the landlord in 1974, when the *Essex and East London News* wrote of the pub, refused to go down the cellar. Many of the customers believe that the strange happenings are connected with the funeral parlour next door, but it seems more likely the terrible events of that night in 1916 caused a disturbance that still has echoes in the psychic world.

Similar disturbances (taps being turned on, etc.) were experienced in the late 1960s in the Nag's Head, Hackney Road. A series of strange, unaccountable mishaps culminated in a cellarman actually seeing the ghost in the cellar. He described it as being a very old woman wearing a grey shawl over a long Victorian dress. Seances were held at the pub, and they seemed to put the ghost to rest.

THE ILLUSTRATED
POLICE News

LAW COURTS AND WEEKLY RECORD

SISTER OF VICTIM

FIFTH VICTIM

MORTUARY

THE BERNER ST. VICTIM.

INSPECTOR REID

INQUEST ON FIFTH VICTIM AT ST GEORGES IN THE EAST

TWO MORE WHITECHAPEL HORRORS. WHEN WILL THE MURDERER BE CAPTURED?

BACK OF BERNER STREET

FIRST DISCOVERY OF THE CRIME

POLICE CONSTABLE WATKINS SIGNALLING FOR ASSISTANCE

MITRE SQUARE ALDGATE

THE FATAL SPOT

GOING TO HER DOOM

FINDING THE BODY IN MITRE SQUARE

THE SCENE ON SUNDAY IN BERNER STREET

INTERIOR OF THE GATE

THE FIFTH VICTIM OF THE WHITECHAPEL FIEND.

FINDING THE MUTILATED BODY

East Enders have always been quick to cash in on slender opportunities and when the landlord of the Ten Bells in Commercial Street, Whitechapel (on the corner with Fournier Street) discovered that the body of the fourth of Jack the Ripper's eight victims had been found close to the back of the pub in Hanbury Street, he changed its name to 'Jack the Ripper'. The walls were decorated with contemporary accounts from the *Police Gazette* and other chronicles of the time, and with a facsimile copy of the original police file on the case. Then they discovered that the name of the Ripper's victim found behind the pub was Emily Annie Chapman – the maiden name of the landlord's wife!

The police never found the Ripper. He committed eight savage murders in the Whitechapel/Hackney area between April 1888 and July 1889. The district was then notorious for its prostitutes, who were far removed from their higher-class sisters who worked the West End. The East End ladies of the street were content to receive the price of a bed in a common boarding-house in exchange for their favours, and Emily Chapman was returning to just such a house when she was attacked. A witness who discovered her body described the horror of the sight:

> Her clothes were thrown back, but her face was visible. Her apron seemed to be thrown back over her clothing. I could see from the feet up to the knees. She had a handkerchief of some kind round her throat . . . it seemed as if her inside had been pulled from her, and thrown at her. It was lying over her left shoulder.

At first, when it was discovered that the woman had been disembowelled, it was thought that the murderer had intended to take away the womb, for which an American university would pay £20. However the injuries of the later victims were not consistent with this pattern, and the police abandoned their theory that the murders were done for gain. The enduring feeling of the local population was that the culprit was a member of the high aristocracy, Royal Family, or Government who was safe from the attentions of the police: after all, what were the deaths of a few ageing prostitutes against the mighty edifice of Victorian respectability?

There is no escaping that the sudden, horrific demise of the Ripper's victims should give rise to ghosts in the dark alleys of Whitechapel, and there were many reports of ghosts here after the murder. The most famous is that immortalised by Elliott O'Donnell –

The Illustrated Police News *on 13 October 1888, reflected the public's growing fascination with the activities of the Ripper.* (BRITISH LIBRARY, COLINDALE)

the 'huddled figure, like that of a woman, emitting from all over it a ghostly light, frequently to be seen lying in the gutter.' This was often seen in Durward Street where the Ripper's first kill, Polly Nicholls, was found. Furthermore the landlord of the 'Jack the Ripper' was quite certain that it was the ghost of Emily Chapman which haunted his pub. Anyway, he managed to get a good mention in the *Hackney Gazette* in August 1975, when he claimed the ghost for his pub, complaining of the strange gusts of cold wind that came from nowhere, and the radio that would switch itself on and off, and other more or less unaccountable happenings that took place there.

In 1979 the *Essex and East London News* reported on a disapproving ghost which haunted the Drivers' Arms, Mile End. The landlady was justifiably upset when her drinks completely vanished (at first she suspected that there was a practical joker among her customers). Then heavy objects began to be dislodged mysteriously, and were seen to move of their own accord. She called in a medium who was able to explain that there was a ghost of a previous, Victorian, tenant who disapproved of women drinking, and because of this caused the trouble.

Another Mile End ghost was unusual in being that of a person still alive. The same newspaper reported on a strange haunting at the Ancient Briton, Glaucas Street. The ghost was again that of a former tenant of the pub who was still alive and well and living in Goodmayes. She had had to leave the pub when her husband died, having spent fourteen enjoyable years there. She was seen in the cellar by the new manager who described the figure in detail to a former barmaid who was able to identify it as being that of the previous landlady.

You would expect the pubs of Dockland to be too busy with drinkers to have time for ghosts, yet both the Connaught Tavern in West Ham, and London's oldest riverside pub – the Gun Tavern at Coldharbour on the Isle of Dogs – are reputed to be haunted.

The Connaught has the ghost of a madwoman who committed suicide there. She was the aunt of the landlord, and after she died the bedroom on the second floor was abandoned as she had left it. Gradually over the years the rumpled sheets on the bed became grey with dirt, and layers of dust covered the entire room. If any room should have a ghost it was this one, and sure enough when three members of the staff did manage to pluck up enough courage to look inside, they saw the old mad woman there, her eyes lit by the wild light of insanity, and her mouth twisted into a leering, wicked shape. All three dashed down the stairs to safety. The ghost has not been seen recently, and the Connaught has had many landlords since the death of the old lady.

In 1965 the *Stratford Express* gave a brief mention to the ghost that haunts one of the bedrooms of the Gun Tavern at Coldharbour. Since Lord Nelson had clandestine meetings with Lady Hamilton here when he returned to land, it is always assumed that his is the ghost that is seen.

On the opposite side of the Isle of Dogs, upriver on Limehouse Reach, passengers on the trip-boats voyaging to Greenwich will see an ancient inscription: 'Site of the building and launching of Steamship "Great Eastern" 1853–8'. Because of the enormous size of the vessel (22,500 tons), Brunel had it built side-on to the river – its passage to the river and launching being controlled by hydraulic rams. Disasters regularly befell the ship during its construction. Four workmen were killed before the launching: one was crushed to death inside the superstructure; another fell to his death on the steel plates of the keel; a young boy working as a riveter's mate also fell and was impaled on a scaffolding support; and one of the 200 riveters disappeared without trace while working on the 3,000,000 hand-driven rivets which held the plates of the hull together – the hull was built with two thicknesses. A sightseer who came to Millwall to stand amazed and in awe at the enormous size of the *Great Eastern* was struck dead by a monkey-wrench which fell from the hand of a workman far above.

The launching of this 'Wonder of the Seas', six times larger than any ship built previously, was scheduled to take place on 3 November 1857, at high tide, which was at midday. Against Brunel's wishes a great crowd assembled to watch the spectacular event. The fastenings at bow and stern were slackened, and a great creaking, groaning sound came from the hull, but though the noise continued for ten minutes the ship failed to move. Then suddenly the slipway shook as she began to slide, taking by surprise the gang of men operating the giant windlass which was meant to control the rate of her descent into the water. Its enormous handles spun madly as the chain ran out, and the inattentive men were flung high into the air by the tremendous force unleashed. One was killed outright and others suffered terrible injury. Spectators on board barges in the river, seeing the monster begin its uncontrolled slide towards them, jumped

The SS Great Eastern. (BRUNEL UNIVERSITY)

into the water in desperate efforts to escape: two were drowned. In fact there was no need for such panic for the great hull came to a standstill before reaching the water, in a great welter of noxious Thames mud.

It took many more months before the gigantic, jinxed ship could be got afloat, and the worries and recriminations finally broke Brunel's failing health. However, early on the morning of 5 September 1859, he came on board the ship in order to select cabins for himself and his family on the maiden voyage. He undertook a final tour of inspection, and having completed this was photographed on board the ship. Within minutes he collapsed with a stroke and was carried ashore to his home; he never arose from his bed again.

The *Great Eastern* put to sea attended by a host of small boats carrying cheering crowds. At six o'clock on the evening of 9 September she was in the Channel abreast of the Dungeness Light, steaming at thirteen knots, when the paddle-wheel boilers blew up, killing six stokers and wrecking much of the superstructure and all of the Grand Saloon. The explosion had been caused by an engineer's negligence in allowing too much steam into the feedwater heaters, but the day before the captain had complained of a constant

hammering that seemed to come from below. The cause of this was never found, yet the hammering always recurred when a mishap was about to hit the vessel. In this instance the hammering heralded not only disaster to the *Great Eastern* but the death of Brunel: he died shortly after being told of the explosion, on 15 September.

The *Great Eastern*'s career was comparatively short. She had been designed to carry a great number of passengers cheaply on lengthy voyages. She would have made an ideal carrier for the thousands of emigrants who were at the time leaving Europe for America and Australia. Brunel had intended her to steam non-stop to Australia. Her owners never used her on this run, persisting in using her as a luxury vessel on the Atlantic – in this role she was an economic disaster, and in the 1860s her luxurious fittings were taken out and she was converted to cable-laying, putting down the first transatlantic telegraph cable between 1865 and 1866. After this her useful life was virtually at an end, and she was scrapped in 1888. On the way to the breaker's yard the unaccountable hammering was heard once more, as it had been before each untoward incident in the past. Shortly afterwards the tow-lines parted and the *Great Eastern* was almost wrecked. When the breakers came to dismantle the mighty hull they found a sealed compartment in the space between the outer and inner shells. In it was a skeleton with an old carpet-bag containing rusty tools. Presumably this was the missing 'rivet-basher' whose ghostly knocking had presaged the disasters which befell the mammoth ship so frequently.

Ten years before the demise of the *Great Eastern* a more tragic accident had occured on the Thames on Barking Reach, a little way downstream from her launching site. In September 1878 the pleasure-steamer *Princess Alice* was rammed by a collier. Cut in two, the *Princess Alice* sank almost immediately and 640 day-trippers died. Many of them were later found not to have drowned but to have been poisoned by the horribly polluted waters (the collision took place close to the outfall of the London drainage system, and in those days sewerage was released untreated into the Thames). The victims' pathetic cries may be heard echoing over the marshes on the anniversary of the incident.

Limehouse, upstream again, was once the roughest area of Dockland. Whores would sell themselves to newly landed sailors for the price of a drink or a 'doss' in a boarding-house. There were lodging-houses for the sailors too, and it is said that one of them was

The last photograph of Isambard Kingdom Brunel taken on board the Great Eastern *minutes before he suffered the stroke that proved fatal.* (BRUNEL UNIVERSITY)

The sinking of the Princess Alice *in September 1878.* (MARY EVANS PICTURE LIBRARY)

run by a clergyman, the Vicar of Ratcliff-Cross. Two hundred years ago he became notorious for murdering his wealthier clients during the night, and dumping their bodies in the river. Many of the old lightermen who used to work this stretch of the river would be reluctant to linger alone on Ratcliff Wharf, even in daylight (for this reason the wharf was always closed at five in the evenings).

In 1971 a building contractor engaged on construction work at the wharf became aware of a little old gentleman watching him at work from about twenty yards away. He was dressed in a strange black costume with a high collar, wore gaiters, and leaned on a cane. His long white hair was blown by the wind and his attention seemed to have been caught by something beyond the builder. The latter looked behind him to see what it was that the old man found so interesting, found nothing, and turned back to the old man. He was no longer there! Yet there was nowhere on that wharf that he could have hidden in those few seconds. He checked the dock, the river, and all around without success. When his three colleagues returned he told them of the mystery and they enjoyed his embarrassment when they started pulling his leg about it. Yet within the next few days all three were witness to a similar apparition, and none of them knew the story of the Vicar of Ratcliff. They were all pleased when their work at the wharf was finished. Locally it is said that the ghost usually appears on summer evenings, though all the 1971 sightings were on Sunday mornings in July.

Sadly this story is, in fact, a hoax dreamed up by Frank Smyth, an Assistant Editor of the part-work *Man, Myth & Magic*. First published in the part-work, it was later faithfully recorded in two books on the ghosts of London before the hoax was revealed in 1978 by Daniel Farson in the *Hamlyn Book of Ghosts*. However even before the tale was printed Smyth was startled to meet a lighterman who told him that the story of a ghostly Vicar of Ratcliff had been known to his family for generations. Was the invented story a residual memory that lurked in his unconscious mind? Fortunately the ghost of the murderous Vicar does not seem to have caught up with its creator, so far. . . .

In this chapter we have already dealt with East End pubs, but not with the haunted brewery office. This is the Bass Sales Office at Cephas Street in Stepney, and the *East London Advertiser* told the story in 1980:

> Staff at a brewery office are getting a terrific draught from the spirit world – and they want to find out why.
>
> For the workers at Bass Sales have been getting a cold sensation at their offices, a former doctor's surgery in Cephas Street, Stepney.
>
> And besides the cold shoulder the sweet sickly smell of embalming fluid has been sending cold shivers up and down their spines.
>
> One of the workers said: 'For the past year the smell has become so apparent it's unnatural.
>
> 'We can be talking about something and then there is a strange cold sensation, which makes the hair on your arms stand on end.'

The only explanation for this put forward was that the office was built on the site of a doctor's surgery, and about forty years ago a pregnant woman had been knocked down outside, and then brought in for medical attention. She had died there, though her baby was saved.

In July 1976, the same newspaper, worthy for the attention it gives the supernatural, reported on strange goings-on in the matron's room at the magistrates' court at Stepney. All sorts of incidents upset the day-to-day routine, caused, the Matron believed, by the old lady who had been her predecessor. This was old Mrs Browne who had worked there for twenty-five years, until she was seventy-seven. She was then taken ill with thrombosis and so had to retire, dying soon after. That had been five years previously, and since then a series of events had led her successor as matron, Mrs Gumbrill, to believe that the place was haunted. Articles often floated across the room, and food trays were sometimes snatched from Mrs Gumbrill's hands and dashed to the floor. Witnesses backed up Mrs Gumbrill's account, but as no sequel to the original account appeared it is not known for how long the ghost remained troublesome.

An unidentified ghost haunted the London Jewish Hospital, Stepney, in 1977. He was taken to be an ex-patient and his 'hazy figure' often visited a day-room used by nurses on night duty when they rest. Nurses were particularly frightened by the ghost brushing past them, and one positively identified him as a patient she had known. Although the Jewish religion has no service of exorcism it was suggested that a rabbi should be invited in to say prayers. Presumably this put the spirit to rest, for there have been no further reports of a sighting from the hospital.

Housing officers on local councils are accustomed to complaints of ghosts, and are generally sceptical when they are accompanied by requests for different accommodation. However not all such complaints are bogus, and undoubtedly many people leading normal untroubled lives can become seriously disturbed by paranormal happenings.

Barton House, Bow, is an ordinary-looking block of flats owned by the GLC. In February 1977, the *East Ender* told how the Ussher family had suffered from the appearance of the ghost of a little old lady wearing carpet slippers and a white apron. She proved to be a mischievous or even malevolent ghost, knocking items from shelves and tampering with electrical fittings. A favourite trick was to plunge the flat into darkness by throwing the mains switch. Exorcism by an Anglican vicar and by a Catholic priest failed to bring release from the old lady: a medium was called in but could only confirm the ghost's hostility to the family. The local librarian found that the flats were built on the site of an ancient convent – but the ghost was never described as being nun-like. The Housing Officer found that the flat had never been occupied by an old lady, but promised to move the Usshers elsewhere when an alternative became available. This story is typical of many, and researchers are always wary of people's motives in reporting seeing a ghost.

The Ghosts of Islington

Pride of place must go to the Islington Ghost itself – Mr Richard Cloudesley. The account is taken from a booklet bearing that title in Islington Library: '. . . being a short account of the burial of a gentleman at Islington with a relation of several strange appearances which followed.' (Muggins & Co., Clerkenwell, 1842.)

> Thus far concerning ghosts in general: we now proceed to speak of the ISLINGTON GHOST. When we consider that this was in our own immediate neighbourhood, we might well be filled with horror, consternation, and dismay, were it not for the assurance that this ghost is now laid. The name of the gentleman whose ghost caused such alarm, was Richard Cloudesley. He was probably of the same family as William Cloudesley, an early benefactor to the parish, and possibly descended from, or in some way connected with William of Cloudesley, a famous archer and outlaw, who at an early period infested the northern counties of England. The aforesaid Mr Richard Cloudesley was an inhabitant of the parish of Saint Mary, Islington, and a considerable landed proprietor. He died in the year 1517, bequeathing to the parish an estate of fourteen acres (commonly called the Stonefield estate) which is

Trinity Church, Cloudesley Square, Islington (it is now the 'Celestial Church of Christ' – a hot-gospel church of the pentecostal variety). (ISLINGTON LIBRARY)

19

Collins' Music Hall c. *1910.* (ISLINGTON LIBRARY)

situated in the Liverpool Road, Trinity Church standing upon a part of it. A window of this Church contains the portrait of Mr Cloudesley in painted glass, which we would respectfully urge our readers to examine upon the first opportunity. But we are imperceptibly diverging from our subject. Mr Cloudesley pursuant to the directions given in his last will was buried in the yard of the parish church. The passage in which these directions are given reads thus:– 'I bequeath . . . my body after I am passed this present and transitory life to be buried within the church-yard of the parish Church of Islington, near unto the grave of my father and mother.' The following epitaph was placed upon his tomb:

'HERE LYES THE BODY OF RICHARD CLOUDESLEY, A GOOD BENEFACTOR TO THIS PARISH, WHO DIED 9 HENRY VIII. ANNO DOMINI, 1517.'

All the provisions made by Mr Cloudesley for his repose would seem from the testimony of a respectable writer to have proved ineffectual. This author, after speaking of certain earthquakes, proceeds as follows:– 'and as to the same heavings, or *tremblements de terre*, it is said that in a certain field, near unto the parish church of Islington, in like manner did take place a wondrous commotion in various parts, the earth swelling, and turning up every side towards the midst of the said field, and by tradition of this, it is observed that one Richard Cloudesley lay buried in or near that place, and that his body being restless, on the score of some sin by him peradventure committed, did shew, or seem to signify, that religious observance should there take place, to quiet his departed spirit; whereupon certain exorcisers (if we may so term them) did at dead of night, nothing loth, using divers exercises at torchlight, set to rest the unruly spirit of the said Cloudesley, and the earth did return to its pristine shape, nevermore commotion proceeding therefrom to this day, and this I know of a very certainty.'

Elsewhere we are told that Richard Cloudesley's ghost was only laid after a thousand Masses were said for his soul. Moreover in 1813 his remains were moved (though without dire consequences apparently) as the inscription shows:

This tomb was erected by an order of Vestry held on Easter Tuesday the 20th Day of April 1813, to perpetuate the memory of Richard Cloudesley, a very considerable benefactor to this parish who was interred AD 1517, whose remains were found and deposited in a leaden coffin underneath on the 10th of June 1813.

Other ghosts of Islington include that of the impresario Sam Collins which used to haunt the Music Hall he once owned on the Green. Sam always used the same seat (Row B, No. 6) and the cleaning women got so used to his being there that they would clean round him. In 1960 he was seen to walk through the wall of the cellar, but there are no accounts of his ghost having appeared since the old building was knocked down, soon afterwards.

No. 113 Bride Street is now a telephone exchange, but once it was a chapel of the Sandemanian sect. Michael Faraday (who discovered the principle of electro-magnetic induction upon which Bell's telephone was dependent) was an elder of this sect, and a plate in the floor of the exchange marks the position of his pew when it was a

Michael Faraday by T. Phillips, 1841–2. (NATIONAL PORTRAIT GALLERY)

chapel. Faraday's ghost has been seen in the building.

The Old Queen's Head on Essex Road has several ghosts. The original pub, whose licence was granted by Sir Walter Raleigh and which was used by Queen Elizabeth herself, was pulled down in 1829. Even then strange stories were told of it: one of its upper rooms was sealed off because children, victims of the Plague, died there in 1665. Landlords of the rebuilt pub have often been troubled by ghosts – some described an Elizabethan lady, others swear that they have seen the sad figure of a little girl. On the first Sunday of every month doors open and close and footsteps are heard coming down the stairs. Legend says that Queen Elizabeth had a tunnel built from the Queen's Head to Canonbury Tower so that she could discreetly visit her lover, the Earl of Essex, there. An enduring theme of the haunting is the sound of a lady's footsteps with the swish of a full-skirted dress.

The Old Queen's Head, Islington. (ISLINGTON LIBRARY)

London North-West

In April 1980 the *St Pancras Chronicle* printed the report of a most curious episode. It concerned an ancient suit of armour that an antique-dealer had in his shop in Grafton Road. He obtained it from a house in Hackney which he had cleared out. After repair the armour (which he discovered was originally from Spain) stood in his shop for several months. Then one day it was spotted by an Arab gentleman who stopped his Rolls-Royce outside and paid the dealer the price he was asking without a quibble.

Soon afterwards the haunting began. A tall, bearded, noble-looking figure began to haunt the shop, a sad expression on his face. His dignity was in no way diminished by the fact that he only wore strange, scanty undergarments. After several meetings with the figure the proprietor decided that the ghost was restless because his armour had been removed. Unfortunately he found that it had already been shipped to the Middle East and so the sad knight continued to walk in the shop in Kentish Town.

Dr Hawley Harvey Crippen was hanged on 23 November 1910 for the savage murder of his wife. The fame of this murder owed more to the manner of the culprit's capture than to the deed itself – he was apprehended on a transatlantic liner with his mistress, the message having been transmitted by 'wireless'. Before the murder he spent many late nights wandering deep in thought around a piece of waste ground close to his house at Hilldrop Crescent, Kentish Town – presumably plotting the way to kill his wife. An investigator of the supernatural thought it worth while to watch here on the night before Crippen's execution. He was rewarded by seeing a phantom figure bearing a strange-looking parcel cross the ground, going towards ancient junk-strewn ponds near by. After a few minutes the ghost returned – without its burden. Mrs Crippen's head and some other portions of her anatomy were never found.

There are reports from other parts of the country of body-snatchers fabricating ghosts so that their own activities might continue undisturbed. This seems not to have happened so much in Central London, though the gang of 'resurrectionists' from St Pancras was probably the busiest of any operating in England. Furthermore one of their company even kept a diary between 1811 and 1812 which was published by the Librarian of the Royal College of Surgeons in 1896.

'Resurrectionists' at work.

These are the entries relating to the old churchyard of St Pancras (which was formerly in Pancras Road):

Feb. 20, 1812. Thursday.
'Met, and went to Pancras, and got 15 large, & 1 small. Took them to Bartholw.'
Mar. 3, 1812. Tuesday.
'Went to St Thomas's, at night went to Pencress, and got 8 adults, 2 small, and 2 foetus.'
Mar. 25, 1812. Wednesday.
'Went to Pencress got 5 adult, Took them to Bartholomew.'
Mar. 31, 1812. Tuesday.
'Went to Pencress, got 5 adults Bill, Ben & me. Dan'l, Jack and Tom went to Harps, missed.'
Nov. 25, 1812. Wednesday.
'Met at Jack at 2 p.m. Butler & myself went to the B. Ln. got 1 adt. Jack, Ben & Bill went to Pancs. got 5 adult, & 1 small. Took them to Bartholw. Removed 3 to Cline, got 2 sets of "cans" [canine teeth].'

Dec. 1, 1812. Tuesday.
'Met at Tottenham Court Road had a dispute in St Ts. Crib. Came home did not do anything, came to the Rockingham Arms, got Drunk.'
Dec. 2, 1812. Wednesday.
'Met at Vickers rectifyd our last account, the party sent out me & Ben to St Thos. Cb. got 1 adt., Bill and Jack Guys Crib 2 adt. but one of them opd. Butler look out for us, took them to St Thos. came home. Met at St Thos. Me & Jack went to Tootm. got 4 adts. Ben and Bill got 6 ad. 1 s. 1 f. at Pancrass took Tootenm. to Wilson, Pans. to Barthol.' (i.e. got 6 adults, 1 small, and 1 foetus from St Pancras: these were taken to St Bartholomew's; the four from Tottenham went to Mr Wilson).

The editor of the diary comments that the gang worked all the public and private graveyards in and around London. They supplied not only hospitals and doctors, but also teeth for use by dentists 'which they drew from bodies that were too decomposed for anatomical investigation'. The teeth, incidentally, were then used for dentures since artificial teeth were not then made.

Stories of the supernatural often embrace witchcraft but this is less common in London where the people have always had a reputation for being less gullible than their country counterparts. An exception is the story of Mother Red Cap of Camden Town, quoted verbatim here from *History of St Pancras*, written in 1870 by Samuel Palmer:

LIFE OF MOTHER DAMNABLE,
THE ORIGINAL MOTHER RED CAP OF CAMDEN TOWN.

This singular character, known as Mother Damnable, is also called Mother Red Cap, and sometimes the Shrew of Kentish Town. Her father's name was Jacob Bingham, by trade a brickmaker in the neighbourhood of Kentish Town. He enlisted in the army, and went with it to Scotland, where he married a Scotch pedlar's daughter. They had one daughter, this Mother Damnable. This daughter they named Jinney. Her father on leaving the army took again to his old trade of brickmaking, occasionally travelling with his wife and child as a pedlar. When the girl had reached her sixteenth year, she had a child by one Coulter, who was better known as Gipsy George. This man lived no one knew how; but he was a great trouble to the

The old 'Mother Red Cap' Inn, 1746. (MANSELL COLLECTION)

magistrates. Jinney and Coulter after this lived together; but stealing a sheep from some lands near Holloway, Coulter was sent to Newgate, tried at the Old Bailey, and hung at Tyburn. Jinney then associated with one Darby; but this union produced a cat and dog life, for Darby was constantly drunk; so Jinney and her mother consulted together, Darby was suddenly missed, and no one knew whither he went. About this time her parents were carried before the justices for practising the black art, and therewith causing the death of a maiden, for which they were both hung. Jinney then associated herself with one Pitcher, though who or what he was, was never known; but after a time his body was found crouched up in the oven, burnt to a cinder. Jinney was tried for the murder, but acquitted because one of her associates proved he had "often got into the oven to hide himself from her tongue."

Jinney was now a lone woman; for her former companions were afraid of her. She was scarcely ever seen, or if she were, it was at nightfall, under the hedges or in the lanes; but how she subsisted was a miracle to her neighbours. It happened during the Commonwealth troubles that a man, sorely pressed by his pursuers, got into her house by the back door, and begged on his knees for a night's lodging. He was haggard in his countenance, and full of trouble. He offered Jinney money, of which he had

Mother Damnable

of KENTISH TOWN

— Anno 1676. —

From a Unique Print in the Collection of I. Bindley Esqr.

Publish'd by I. Caulfield 1793.

plenty, and she gave him a lodging. This man, it is said, lived with her many years, during which time she wanted for nothing, though hard words and sometimes blows were heard from her cottage. The man at length died, and an inquest was held on the body; but though every one thought him poisoned, no proof could be found, and so she escaped harmless.

After this Jinney never wanted money, as the cottage she lived in was her own, built on waste land by her father.

Years thus passed, Jinney using her foul tongue against every one, and the rabble in return baiting her as if she were a wild beast. The occasion of this arose principally from Jinney being reputed a practiser of the black art—a very witch. She was resorted to by numbers as a fortune-teller and healer of strange diseases; and when any mishap occurred, then the old crone was set upon by the mob and hooted without mercy. The old, ill-favoured creature would at such times lean out of her hatch-door, with a grotesque red cap on her head. She had a large broad nose, heavy, shaggy eyebrows, sunken eyes, and lank and leathern cheeks; her forehead wrinkled, her mouth wide, and her looks sullen and unmoved. On her shoulders was thrown a dark grey striped frieze, with black patches, which looked at a distance like flying bats. Suddenly she would let her huge black cat jump upon the hatch by her side, when the mob instantly retreated from a superstitious dread of the double foe.

The extraordinary death of this singular character is given in an old pamphlet—"Hundreds of men, women, and children were witnesses of the devil entering her house in his very appearance and state, and that, although his return was narrowly watched for, he was not seen again; and that Mother Damnable was found dead on the following morning, sitting before the fire-place, holding a crutch over it, with a tea-pot full of herbs, drugs, and liquid, part of which being given to the cat, the hair fell off in two hours, and the cat soon after died; that the body was stiff when found, and that the undertaker was obliged to break her limbs before he could place them in the coffin, and that the justices have put men in possession of the house to examine its contents."

Such is the history of this strange being, whose name will ever be associated with Camden Town, and whose reminiscence will ever be revived by the old wayside house, which, built on the site of the old beldame's cottage, wears her head as the sign of the tavern.

Highgate

A featherless chicken would seem to make an unlikely ghost, yet it is this that has haunted Pond Square for hundreds of years, since Francis Bacon, a Lord Chancellor of England and extraordinary man of science, undertook his final experiment in 1626. The account is from John Aubrey's *Anecdotes*:

His lordship was trying an experiment, as he was taking the aire with Doctor Witherborne, a Scotchman, physitian to the king, towards Highgate. Snow lay upon the ground; and it came into my Lord's thoughts why flesh might not be preserved in Snow as in salt. They were resolved they would try the experiment presently; they alighted out of the Coach, and went into a poor woman's House, at the bottom of Highgate Hill, and bought a hen, and made the woman exenterate it, and then stuffed the bodie with snow; and my lord did help to do it himself. The snow so chilled him, he immediately fell so ill that he could not return to his lodging (I suppose then at Gray's Inn), but went to the Earl of Arundel's house at Highgate, where they put him into a good bed warmed with a panne; but it was a damp bed, that had not been layn about a yeare before, which gave him such a cold, that in two or three days he died of suffocation.

The following is a copy of Lord Bacon's last letter to the Earl of Arundel and Surrey:—

'MY VERY GOOD LORD,—I was likely to have had the fortune of Caius Plinius the elder, who lost his life by trying an experiment about the burning of Mount Vesuvius; for I was also desirous to try an experiment or two touching the conservation and induration of bodies. As for the experiment itself, it succeeded excellently well; but in the journey between London and Highgate, I was taken with such a fit of casting as I know not whether it were the Stone, or some surfeit or cold, or indeed a touch of them all three. But when I came to your Lordship's House, I was not able to go back, and therefore was forced to take up my lodging here, where your housekeeper is very careful and diligent about me, which I assure myself your Lordship will not only pardon towards him, but think the better of him for it. For indeed your Lordship's House was happy to me, and I kiss your noble hands for the welcome which I am sure you give me to it, etc.

'I know how unfit it is for me to write with any other hand than mine own, but by my troth my fingers are so disjointed with sickness that I cannot steadily hold a pen.'

Perhaps the poor bird knew that in the twentieth century millions of its kind would be bred to meet their ends in a similar way without ever experiencing a natural life. The macabre carcass, flapping stumpy wings, has appeared far less frequently in recent years, and its frantic squawks are no longer heard.

Ye Olde Gate House pub is at the top of Highgate Hill: in the days of the cattle-drovers it would be the last resting-place for men and beasts before they reached Smithfield the next day. Its history goes back to 1310 when it received its first licence. The ghost is that of an old lady, Mother Marnes, who was killed here (with her pet cat) for her money. The black-robed figure still haunts the pub, though it never appears if children or animals are in the building.

Elthorne Road is at the bottom of Highgate Hill, and the occupants of a three-year-old GLC flat in Beechcroft Way close by were greatly troubled by poltergeist activity in 1978. Heavy objects were seen to be moved by invisible means, and the vague outline of a figure was seen, not only by the couple living in the flat but by several of their neighbours as well. In this case the occupants stressed that they had no wish to move, as they had spent a lot decorating and furnishing the flat. Things quietened down after a service of blessing was held.

Highgate Cemetery has long had the reputation of being one of the most haunted, evil places in London. Its array of ornate sarcophagi, monuments and dark vaults evoke the feeling of a menacing presence which waits to envelop the unwary soul.

One of the earliest of the strange incidents that have taken place her was the disinterment of Elizabeth Siddal, a woman of distinctive beauty who was the favourite model for the Pre-Raphaelite painter, Dante Gabriel Rossetti. Later he married her and was heart-broken when she died in 1862 at the age of twenty-nine. As a gesture of love, he placed a manuscript volume of poems in her coffin. The death of Elizabeth marked a watershed in Rossetti's life – from then on his reputation was in decline, both as an artist (he believed that he was going blind) and as a writer.

He had engaged a ruthless entrepreneur, Charles Augustus Howell, as his literary agent. Howell also handled the work of Ruskin and Swinburne (the latter calling him 'the vilest wretch I ever came

Elizabeth Siddal (MANSELL COLLECTION)

across'), and after years of persuasion he managed to get Rossetti to agree to the opening of Elizabeth Siddal's grave at Highgate in order to retrieve the unpublished poems – 'The Book from the Grave'. This was done on a cold, damp autumn night – 5 October 1869 – by the light of a huge bonfire which soon disclosed that in death Elizabeth's hair was as golden and glorious as it had been when she was alive (it was also considerably longer). The poems were retrieved, disinfected and published soon afterwards. Before the opening of the grave, Rossetti had taken himself off to Scotland where he began to drink the terrible mixture of chloral and whisky which ensured that none of his later work showed the genius of his youth, and brought about an early death.

Neither did Howell fare much better. In 1890 his body was found in the gutter outside a Chelsea public house. His throat had been cut

The Gatehouse and Highgate Village (GUILDHALL LIBRARY)

and a gold coin was between his clenched teeth. The murderer was never found, though for many years Howell's financial affairs had been so disastrous that he had been forced to make a premature announcement of his own death!

Access to Highgate Cemetery is now difficult, due partly to the activities of a self-styled vampire-hunter, Allan Farrant, and his followers in the early 1970s. In August 1970 the *North London Press* reported the first of many disturbances at the cemetery:

> Police are investigating the possibility that the headless body found in Highgate Cemetery last week may have been used in Black Magic rites. Two young girls made the gruesome discovery of a charred woman's body – minus head – as they walked through the cemetery on Friday last week. The body, which had been buried in 1926, came from a family vault in the catacombs of the old cemetery.
>
> 'The body had been charred. It was very well preserved, like a fossil', a police spokesman said.

Two weeks later the *Islington Gazette* carried the story of Farrant's appearance in court, where a large wooden cross, a piece of rope and a crucifix were produced in evidence. He was found guilty of being in St Michael's churchyard for an unlawful purpose, but this seems not to have deterred him, as in the following October he was interviewed by the same newspaper and told them how he and his colleagues of the British Occult Society kept watch over the cemetery at night as they were convinced of a vampire's presence there. Many graves had been smashed and corpses dispersed. In 1973 the *Hornsey Journal* carried an account of more weird goings-on:

> A cat was sacrificed to a horned god in a macabre night-ritual at Highgate Woods during the weekend involving eight hooded coven members and a naked High Priestess who left at the scene a bloodstained carving knife, blood-spattered stockings, and offal. . . .

Farrant's downfall came in the following year: the trial received great publicity at the time. He was sent to gaol for four years and eight months after being found guilty on the following counts: unlawfully and maliciously damaging a memorial to the dead; unlawfully entering a place of interment and interfering with a body; threatening two detectives by sending them voodoo death-spell dolls to prevent or dissuade them from giving evidence in criminal proceedings against fellow occultists, etc. He was also alleged to have conducted Black Magic ceremonies in a vault in which a pretty French girl danced naked over desecrated coffins. The Judge, Michael Argyle, spoke of the horror of the case in his summing-up: 'We were unfortunate enough to have to look at a corpse which had been horribly interfered with on the previous evening. The body had been laying in her coffin since 1884. The tomb had been smashed open and the corpse mutilated.'

The *Islington Gazette* of 2 August 1974, carried an amusing postscript to the story concerning the dolls that had been sent to intimidate the police:

> The dolls had been carefully made in the shape of a grown man – each with an outsize phallus. During their journey through the post, however, the phallic symbols had fallen off.
>
> For weeks leading up to the trial the two detectives had to endure certain embarrassing questions from their colleagues. Word quickly got around the office and even blushing typists and wives were let in on the leg-pull.
>
> The two detectives are happy to report that they are fit and well and that they have nothing amiss to report.

Highgate Cemetery today.

There are more orthodox supernatural activities that occur in the cemetery apart from those involving voodoos and vampires. An old madwoman distractedly searches among the tombs for the children she once murdered; a tall man with a black hat mysteriously fades into the walls of the cemetery at Swain's Lane; and a ghost with bony fingers lurks near the main entrance.

A classic Victorian ghost story was printed in the short-lived *Mother Shipton's Miscellany* on 2 December 1878. Since it concerns Highgate it is reprinted here:

THE SPECTRAL VISITANT,
Or, THE STUDENT'S DEATH BED.

A Narrative founded on facts.
"Truth is strange, stranger than fiction."

HIGHGATE still rejoices in many quaint old mansions, any one of which might possess its own peculiar ghost; rambling red-brick houses, with moss-grown courtyards in front, and spacious yet gloomy apartments, and with gardens stretching far and wide, which with their wealth of sombrous trees and thick plantations, have a stately and mournful aspect. But the house in which the scene of this narrative is laid has gone the way of many a fine suburban residence. The ivy covered walls, worthy of a medieval castle; the massive gates, rust-eaten by age; the broad flight of steps, the richly carved doorway; the spacious marble staircase; the rambling out-houses, each larger than a modern villa; the great bell that clanged the announcement of a new arrival; the terrace walks, with their curiously clipt yews and gardening of a by-gone age; the thatched summer-house, with geometric floor and seats and tables, from which far-reaching views over a smiling landscape were obtained—all, all have gone. But the memory of the strange history now to be related still remains; and "I tell the tale as 'twas told to me."

Wild and reckless had been the youth of the only son and heir of Mr. ——, who lived at the Big House at Highgate—as I shall prefer to call it. He had been away for nearly two years; his name was never mentioned by his stern and high-minded father, and but in hushed whispers by his broken-hearted mother and sisters. But as the Christmas of 1790 approached he came home—as people said, to die.

A nurse was engaged—one of a trusty nature; and one evening a rickety hackney coach toiled up the steep hill, and deposited the worthy woman at the Big House, much agitated by an adventure in the Hollow Way, not unfrequent in those days—the stoppage of the coach by a highwayman near what is now known as Red Cap lane. But the highwayman was in good humour, and after frightening Nurse terribly by strange oaths, let the jarvie drive on, with a warning to have a richer fare next time he ventured on the great North road. As Nurse was shown into the room she shuddered involuntarily: the oak panelling was black with age; the fireplace was supported by massive buttresses, the bed seemed as large as a moderate-sized room. There was but the glimmer of a single lamp in the fireplace, which served only to make darkness visible. The Doctor was just leaving as the good woman arrived, and as he left he enjoined absolute silence. Nurse sat down, replenished the fire, and commenced reading a book of devotion. Now and again, a blast of wind shook the leafless branches of the great elms, while the snow—which had begun to fall—spluttered on the embers as it was wafted down the wide chimney, and gradually wrapt the gardens in a shroud. Curious to see her patient, Nurse gently opened the curtains: contrary to her expectations, he was not asleep, but lay motionless on his back, his bright blue eyes glaring fixedly upon her, his under-lip fallen, and his mouth apart, his cheek a perfect hollow, and his long white teeth projecting fearfully from his shrunken lips, whilst his bony hand, covered with wiry sinews, was stretched upon the bedclothes, and looked more like the claw of a bird than the fingers of a human being. Nurse quietly retired, and two hours passed heavily away. About midnight the patient began to breathe heavily, and appeared very uneasy; turning to look towards him, she was surprised to see a lady closely veiled, seated on a chair near the head of the bed beside him. Nurse though startled was about moving to the bed when the lady with her gloved hand motioned her to keep her seat. Nurse obeyed, but the more she reflected as to how the strange visitor had entered, the more perplexed she became. The shape and turn of her head and neck were graceful in the extreme; the rest of her person she could not so well discern. She at length concluded that the visitor must be some relative of the young man's, although she had been told that the apartment was some distance from the other living rooms. With the curiosity inherent in her sex, she determined to watch the stranger, who continued gazing on the patient, who heaved and sighed and breathed in agony, as if a night-mare were upon him. Nurse again moved towards the bedside, but was again motioned off. Strangely fascinated, she complied, though against her will; and her eyes closing for a moment (for she was fatigued by her journey) she opened them to find the lady gone, and the young man breathing more freely.

Nurse was at her post the next night, but was naturally somewhat nervous. The same scene was enacted. The strange lady entered, how she knew not. As Nurse advanced towards the

Highgate Cemetery (GUILDHALL LIBRARY)

bedside—undeterred by the repellent action of the stranger, the latter withdrew to the table. The thundering clap of a distant door alarmed poor Nurse, more terrified still by the countenance of the patient; big drops of cold sweat were rolling down his pale brow; his livid lips were quivering with agony; and as he motioned her aside, his glaring eyes followed the retreating figure of the lady. Piqued at the young man's refusal of her attentions, she retired in dudgeon; again determined to watch the departure of her mysterious companion, again was she baffled. Sinking to slumber, she was only awoke by the female who had come to relieve her watch. If the room had looked dismal as the flickering fire-light filled it with fantastic shadows, it looked miserable as the dazzling whiteness of the reflected snow outside showed its dirty and dilapidated condition.

The next night was Christmas Eve. Nurse had made up her mind to leave; but the medical man represented how much inconvenience such a course would cause, and pooh-poohed the idea of the occurrence being supernatural in its character, which the old woman began now—with all her piety—to suspect. Nurse accordingly consented to remain; and commenced to watch—not merely the departure but the arrival of her fair friend. The night was stormy, the dry crisp sleet hissed on the window, whilst the wind soughed among the trees like the agonizing wails of lost spirits, and the rattling of ill-secured shutters echoed fearsomely along the dismal passages of the Great House. But as the strange visitant had not appeared on former occasions till the night was far advanced, she now did not expect her sooner, and endeavoured to occupy her attention till that time by some other means. The

occasional ticking of the death-watch; the dull falling of masses of snow from the branches to the ground, all the slight sounds of the sick room, were intensified to Nurse's imagination. She closed her eyes with a feeling of pain; when she opened them, the singular being was there! Again the same distressing scene ensued, her suffering charge gasped and heaved till the noise of his agony made her heart sicken within her; when she drew near the bed his corpse-like features were horribly convulsed and his ghastly eyes straining from their sunken sockets. She spoke, but he answered not; she touched him, but he was cold with terror, and unconscious of any object save the one mysterious being whom his glance followed with a fixed intensity, and who had moved silently away towards the table. Thinking the young man was about expiring, Nurse prepared to leave the room for further assistance, when she saw the lady again move towards the bed of the dying man: she bent over him for a moment, whilst his writhings were indescribable; she then moved statelily towards the door. Now was the moment! Nurse advanced at the same time, laid her one hand on the lock, whilst with the other she attempted to raise the veil of the stranger. The next instant she fell lifeless on the floor. As she glanced on the face of the lady, she saw that a lifeless head filled the bonnet; its vacant sockets and ghastly teeth were all that could be seen beneath the folds of the veil.

Daylight was breaking on the Christmas morning, when the poor old woman, cold and benumbed, was found stretched on the floor of the passage. The invalid lay stiffened and lifeless: one hand thrown across his eyes, as if to shade them from some object on which he feared to look; the other grasping the coverlet with convulsive firmness.

That Christmas morning the body of a woman—young and beautiful—was washed ashore hard by Queenhithe. It had apparently been in the water three or four days. Letters found in her pocket showed conclusively her connection with the young man at the Big House. The family soon deserted the mansion, after pensioning the old Nurse, who, however, never recovered from the shock.

This is the tale; we repeat, a true one, if the solemn asseverations of a Christian woman drawing near her end have any weight. The exact measure of that young man's sin was never known. That its punishment was terrible, this narrative at least has demonstrated.

'. . . a lifeless head filled the bonnet; its vacant 41
sockets and ghastly teeth were all that could
be seen beneath the folds of the veil.' (LONDON
DUNGEON)

Hampstead

The following appeared in the *St James's Gazette*, January 1889:

EXORCISING A GHOST AT HAMPSTEAD.

Miss Frith, daughter of the well-known artist, who writes under the signature "Walter Powell" in a Canadian paper, tells in a recent letter the following version of the ghosts at Hampstead:—

There are two rows of old red brick houses at Hampstead, forming an avenue to the church, which houses, built on ground which once belonged to a monastery, are continually troubled by the most unaccountable noises, in one or two cases the inhabitants declaring that the noises, which they *can* bear, have been further supplemented by the appearance of apparitions, which they *cannot*. Not long ago one of those possessing the worst of reputations was taken in all innocence by some people who, till they had been in the place sometime, were left unmolested. But very soon steps pattered up and down stairs in the dead of night; doors, previously locked, unaccountably flew open; often there was a feeling, even in the broad daylight, that one was being watched (said my informant) by invisible eyes, touched by invisible fingers. The maids gave warning continually, the children occasionally were frightened, but as months went on without anything actually being seen, the footsteps and rustlings, growing monotonous, were at last almost

Church Row, Hampstead.

unheeded, and the household settled down with the firm determination, annoying enough to the ghost, to ignore its presence altogether, a resolution not always strictly kept. One afternoon a November or two ago, the lady of the house sat by the fire in a small drawing-room, shut off from a larger one by folding doors, reading fairy tales to her little daughter, and as she read she heard some one walking overhead, in a room from which the ghost always started on its peregrinations. She glanced at the child, who was staring at the flames absorbed in the history of "The Snow Queen" and who, wisely enough, had no ears for anything else, and continued the story without a pause. Soon on each of the shallow oak stairs sounded the well-known pit-a-pat of high-heeled shoes, till the steps, staying a second at the smaller drawing-room, went on to the larger room, the door of which opened and shut with a bang; but nothing disturbed the little girl. As her mother read on, someone behind those folding doors was turning the handles softly, pacing up and down the floor, moving chairs and small tables, till at last the reader became so nervous she thought she even should have screamed. Instead of that, however, she made some excuse of resting for a moment, gave the book to her daughter, and taking up a lamp went bravely to the threshold of the other room and looked in. The footsteps ceased suddenly, but peer as she might into every corner, nothing could she see. Just as she was turning back to "The Snow Queen" and the fire, the child ran towards her. "Why, mamma," she said, pointing to a window seat on which the stream of lamplight fell brightest, "who is that pretty lady?" Since then Mrs. S., who is a Catholic, has had that restless ghost laid (this is the nineteenth century, five miles from Charing Cross), and with bell and book the priest and the acolyte have done their best to restore peace to No. —, Church row, the consequence being that after that afternoon, spent in sprinklings and prayer, the pretty lady has altogether ceased her visits.

Later accounts, most probably concerning the same ghost, explain that the footsteps were those of a child being pursued. These would stop suddenly and then would come a long, shuddering, sigh. September was the favourite month for the haunting to occur. Dawn would occasionally show the sinister figure of a red-haired serving-maid creeping from the house carrying a carpet-bag. Long ago, it was believed, she had murdered a child who was in her care, dismembered its body, and furtively left the house at first light with the remains in the bag.

The notebooks of John Emslie supply another ghost of this locality:

Mr Ashley, a student at Heatherley's Art Academy, and who lived for two years at the Priory at Hampstead, told me that the latter building was erected by a public-house auctioneer of the name of Thompson who, being supposed from his business to know every corner of a street, was called Corner Thompson: having, in his business capacity, acquired a great many oddities, he erected the odd-looking building (Priory) and furnished it equally oddly: his two daughters married, and one of them is said to have been immured in the walls of the house, and her ghost has been sometimes seen.

Emslie was told this tale in about 1880.

Dick Turpin figures prominently in Hampstead ghost stories. Mounted on his famous black horse, he has often been seen in the vicinity of the Vale of Health. The notorious highwayman gallops up at a furious pace, and just as you feel certain that you will be run down, he vanishes. Before the Second World War the clatter of Black Bess's hoofs was sometimes heard at the famous Spaniards Inn, on the Hampstead Heath, where he used to lodge.

Another ghost from about the same era was as recently as late 1980 experienced by the singer Lynsey de Paul, dining, appropriately, at Turpin's on Heath Road with James Coburn. John Blake, writing in the *New Standard*, quoted her as saying:

All of a sudden I said to James: 'There's a ghost here.' I felt she was a young woman who was strangled in the building in the 1700s. I told a waiter, and he said a girl was stabbed there long ago. Then he came back a few minutes later to tell me he had the story wrong. The girl had been strangled, as I originally thought.

Mr Michael Best, who co-runs the restaurant, told me: 'Lynsey is right – and she couldn't have known about the story beforehand. We took over the restaurant a year ago and heard the tale from an American tourist who lived in the building during the war and witnessed numerous sightings.

'Lynsey was sitting at Table Number Three, near the old fireplace. People have asked to be moved from there in the past because it made them feel uncomfortable.'

Turpin at work.

The William IV pub, in Heath Street, has a ghost which haunts the road outside. A girl in a white shroud and with long plaited hair is seen at the windows, sorrowfully staring in. She is said to be the shade of a young girl who committed suicide in the dentist's surgery that once stood opposite the pub. On the heath itself is a Whistling Stone that marks the spot where a highwayman was killed.

The Northern Suburbs

Bruce Castle, at Tottenham, is now a museum: once it was the home of Rowland Hill, the founder of the penny post and of the British Post Office. Thus it is appropriate that it now displays interesting items connected with the development of the postal system. The building itself dates from Elizabethan times when it was a manor-house. An earlier house was built by the father of Robert Bruce whose family owned the manor of Tottenham in early medieval times.

The mansion's ghost is that of Constantia, the beautiful wife of Lord Coleraine, who was so possessive that he kept her locked up in the small chamber high above the entrance porch. On 3 November 1680, she jumped to her death from the balustrade with her baby in her arms. Her terrible scream was heard on the anniversary of the sad event until early in this century, when a local vicar held a prayer meeting in the room in an attempt to quieten the ghost.

Recent reports of ghosts at Bruce Castle include a lively cavalcade of figures in eighteenth-century costume seen in the grounds in 1971. These ephemeral party-goers appeared twice within a week or so. On the second occasion the couple who saw the gathering approached it, whereupon the figures 'melted into the wall'.

J. P. Emslie was an enthusiastic collector of the folk-tales and traditions of London: his notebooks covered the period between 1860 and 1893 and show a particular interest in ghost stories. The notebooks were edited by F. Celoria for the first issue of *London Studies* in 1974, and are the source for the following stories.

Honeypot Lane, Stanmore, was the scene of a great battle when Caesar's armies first came to Britain. This is said to be the cause of its haunting – for a great rushing sound is sometimes heard on dark nights, and many have spoken of something horrible brushing past them at the same time. Old Church Farm, also at Stanmore, was once a rectory:

People have often seen a ghost rise out of a grave in the field opposite to the farm, go over to the farm, enter it, and come back and re-enter its grave. People have heard knocking, and all kinds of noises: last year a man was in the house, watching a dying woman; no other people were in the house. He saw the parson's ghost come into the room, lean over the woman and look at her, and then retire.

The district around Kingsbury Green and The Hyde at Colindale was haunted by the ghost of a haymaker who had quarrelled with a fellow worker and been fatally stabbed with a pitchfork. The ghost was supposed to be dangerous, and if you encountered it you ran the risk of being run through – with the pitchfork. Hyde Lane was also the haunt of a ghostly donkey, remarkable for being polychromatic, dazzling the beholder with its rainbow colours as it passed.

Another well-haunted thoroughfare, according to Emslie, is Colindeep Lane. The wife of Jack Griffiths drowned herself in a pond by the lane, and it is her ghost that is seen. She was ill-used by her husband, and was 'maddened by drink' when she threw herself in the pond. Another ghost was seen by a policeman in the lane one night, going towards Hendon:

> He saw a man a little in front of him, and walked faster to catch up to him, for the sake of having his company. Not catching the man, he went on increasing his speed until he was running hard, and yet could never catch the man, who suddenly disappeared. The policeman was so frightened, that his hair stood up on end to that extent, that it lifted his hat off his head, and a few days after he died of fright.

In the days when Edmonton was a village, it had a haunted house called 'Wire Hall'. A cook once employed there had murdered a fellow servant. The room where the murder took place was so badly haunted that it had to be bricked up and remained so for fifty years until the house was pulled down. A spectral white dog also haunted this locality (close to Edmonton Church) which never harmed anyone who met with it as long as they ignored it. Another ghost is that of a labourer killed by a bullock at Wire Hall.

Nether Street, West Finchley, was haunted by the ghost of a white lady who frightened many of the local constabulary. One policeman became so preoccupied with the ghost after he had seen it that he spent much time '. . . reading all about the ghosts in the *History of Finchley* until he lost his reason. He is now in an asylum.'

Emslie was a wonderful collector of story and anecdote. A final extract from his work is this opinion, from another policeman:

> A policeman at Bedfont told me something to the following effect: it is written that the time will come when we shall not know night from day, summer from winter, and that when those things shall

A white dog is said to haunt the district around Edmonton church. (GUILDHALL LIBRARY)

come we may look for the end of the world; it does seem as if that time were coming, as the winters have lately been so mild, that workmen used to look to begin working again in the fields as soon as possible after Christmas, but now they look to be keeping at work in the fields up till Christmas time; extologers [*sic*] tell us that as the former world was destroyed by water, the present one will be destroyed by fire, about the year AD 2000, and it does seem as if the world were getting wicked enough for it, for you find that little children damn and bugger, and know as much as grown-up people.

Avenue House, East End Road, Finchley, now houses local government offices. It was once the home of 'Inky' Stephens, manufacturer of pens and ink, who gave the property to Finchley Council. During the war one of the upstairs rooms was converted into a dormitory for women working the switchboard. This was unsuccessful because of a ghost who constantly disturbed the girls sleeping there, always approaching one particular bed, having entered the room without opening the door. After a little it would leave the room in the same way.

Lawrence Street, Mill Hill, was troubled by the activities of a ghost in 1963 after men working in the grounds of St Joseph's Nursing College accidentally unearthed a coffin which turned out to contain the remains of a nun buried in the nineteenth century.

Several housewives living in the vicinity had strange experiences shortly afterwards. Two spoke of seeing a cloaked figure in the street which disappeared as it was approached. They, with several other people living near by, also said that they heard hymn-singing in their houses. At first they thought that this came from their radios, but in all cases their sets turned out to be switched off. A cloaked figure had previously haunted Lawrence Street in the 1920s but the reason for its presence was never discovered.

Leaving the far northern suburbs, and turning east, we come to the fire station at Ilford. Originally this was situated in the Broadway, where in Victorian times Geoffrey Netherwood was one of the firemen. In his spare time he enjoyed reading of the supernatural, which appeared to be his only interest apart from his duties at the fire station. He was well regarded by his colleagues, and when he died his coffin was borne by them to the grave; his gleaming brass helmet was buried with him. Shortly afterwards these same colleagues encountered his ghost in the building, and even in modern times, with the brigade depot having been moved to Romford Road, Geoffrey Netherwood continues to haunt it, still resplendent in his old-fashioned uniform.

In the early years of the present century Perryman's Farm, Ilford, was troubled by a poltergeist which caused damage by breaking crockery and dislodging pictures from the wall. The old lady who lived there resorted to traditional means in order to placate the troubled spirit: each night she left it a bottle of beer and a plate of food on the table. The account fails to tell us whether this generous treatment was successful.

A very traditional English haunting occurs in Bell Lane, Enfield. This is the appearance of the phantom stage-coach known as the 'Enfield Flyer' which strikes terror into the hearts of those it encounters when it dashes towards them out of the darkness. Just as they feel certain that it will run them over it vanishes. Since it seems to travel about five or six feet above the surface of the road, 'run over' is a literal expression. The coach is black and carries two lady passengers wearing large hats. Only a theoretical explanation for this haunting has ever been given: which is, that in olden days the level of the road was higher as the surrounding land had not been drained and was often flooded; the coach and its occupants may have come to disaster when it crashed off the road into the flood waters of the River Lea (the phantom coach has also been seen to vanish into this river).

Wanstead churchyard provides the frightening spectacle of a ghostly skeleton wheeling the coffin cart. As it approaches an ornate tomb, a spectre in white emerges and passionately embraces the bony frame. Do not be alarmed, though, as it is a family reunion – the ghosts are man and wife!

Singular Execution of the Countess of Salisbury in 1541.

The Spectres of the Tower

This, the capital's foremost historical attraction, has a legacy of horror and suffering extending to comparatively recent times. The Romans placed a fortification here when they founded the city, principally to protect the approach to the city upriver from the sea. Parts of the walls they built to enclose their settlement are incorporated into the defences of the Tower and may still be seen today, but the main work dates from 1078, William the Conqueror also appreciating the strategic value of the site. Many of his successors put up further defence-works to make it even more secure, necessary as weapons became more sophisticated. Living quarters were also made more elaborate until the Tower eventually became a town within a town – its life revolving round that of its most important citizen, at many times throughout history the monarch himself.

At the hub of the fortress is the Conqueror's White Tower: the defences surrounding it were designed for two functions – not only should they keep the enemy at bay, but they should also serve to make escape impossible for the prisoners held within. Many of the most illustrious figures of our history have been confined in the Tower's lodgings and dungeons: once incarcerated in the Tower most of them knew that their fate was already determined; even though execution might be delayed for many years, in most cases political expediency made the monarch sign the fatal decree in the end.

Execution by the axeman's hand at the block on Tower Green would have been a welcome end to the suffering of many held captive here. Terrible instruments of torture were used to extract confessions from prisoners, and many suffered the greatest agonies without repudiating their allegiance or faith. Thus it can hardly come as a surprise that the sufferings of these poor souls live on at the Tower in the psychic plane. For the variety of its manifestations it is unrivalled in Britain and, most probably, anywhere in the world. They are dealt with more comprehensively in G. Abbott's excellent *Ghosts of the Tower of London*, published in 1980, and only a select few can be mentioned here.

Even as recently as the time of the Second World War the Tower was used as a prison. Spies and traitors were kept safe behind its massive walls, and a few of them met their ends facing a firing-squad close to the Traitors' Gate. Quite recently a yeoman warder, looking from the window of his house one evening, was startled to see a strange figure suddenly appear only yards from the old shooting-range where executions took place. The man, his head bowed, was dressed in a drab grey utility suit of the 1940s. As the warder strained his eyes to try to take in more details the figure vanished.

One evening in 1954, at fifteen minutes before midnight, a sentry saw a puff of white smoke come from the barrel of one of the ancient cannon that abound at the Tower. This lingered for a moment, then made the shape of a square and began to drift towards the guardsman, changing shape again as it did so. At this the sentry left the scene to fetch a colleague, and when he returned both saw the smoke 'dangling on the wrong side of the steps leading to the top of the wall'. The strange mass quivered in constant movement, but by the time the guard was turned out all trace of it had vanished. (*Proceedings of the Society for Psychical Research*, **53**, 150.)

The Traitors' Gate was the watergate entrance for prisoners condemned after trial at Westminster. It dates from 1240 when Henry III enlarged the fortress by building outer defence-works. There is a story that when work on the gate was almost complete a great storm undermined the foundations on St George's Day 1240, with the result that the gate collapsed. When the circumstances were repeated identically the following year an inquiry revealed that a priest claimed to have witnessed the ghost of St Thomas Becket striking the stonework with a crucifix, lamenting that the new defence-works were not for the common good but 'for the injury and prejudice of the Londoners, my brethren'. Since it was the King's grandfather who had caused the death of the Saint he felt it politic to include a small oratory in the tower of the new building dedicated to St Thomas Becket. Even so its rooms have always had the reputation of being haunted. Doors open and close without reason, the figure of a monk in a brown robe has been seen, and ghostly footsteps – the distinctive 'slap' of monastic sandals – are sometimes heard. As in many different parts of the Tower, these rooms also occasionally echo with the agonised groans and shrieks of long-dead prisoners suffering duress, but perhaps the saddest sounds of all are the heart-rending sobs of a baby that died centuries ago.

Only a few of the ghosts can be readily identified. Henry VI was stabbed to death, most probably by Richard, Duke of York (later King Richard III), during the hour before midnight on 21 May 1471. The chamber where this awful deed took place is reputed to be haunted by

'The Night before the Execution' by George Cruikshank. (BRITISH LIBRARY)

the figure of the victim which always appears at this time.

Anne Boleyn, the most celebrated of the wives of Henry VIII, was beheaded on Tower Green in 1536. Her ghost has frequently been seen both on the Green and, more spectacularly, in the Chapel Royal situated in the White Tower. Here a Captain of the Guard saw a light burning in the locked chapel late at night. Finding a ladder, he was able to use it to look down on the strange scene being enacted within. A nineteenth-century account described it thus:

> Slowly down the aisle moved a stately procession of knights and ladies, attired in ancient costumes; and in front walked an elegant female whose face was averted from him, but whose figure greatly resembled the one he had seen in reputed portraits of Anne Boleyn. After having repeatedly paced the chapel, the entire procession, together with the light, disappeared.
> (*Ghostly Visitors* by 'Spectre Stricken', London 1882.)

Another account of this story tells how the procession always occurs on the anniversary of the terrible execution of the Countess of

Salisbury in 1541. This brave old lady (she was over seventy at the time of her death) suffered because of her son's (Cardinal Pole) vilification of Henry VIII's religious doctrines, a campaign the Cardinal conducted from the safety of France. Thus his mother was brought to the block by Henry as an act of vengeance, but instead of submitting meekly to the axeman she refused to lay down her head and was pursued round the scaffold by him. Swinging wildly he inflicted the most hideous wounds on his victim till she at last succumbed. This event may also be the cause of the sinister shadow of an axe which passes over Tower Green before becoming clearly defined on the wall of the White Tower, where it stands 'menacingly erect'.

A further sighting of the ghost of Anne Boleyn is contained in the proceedings of a court martial that took place in 1864. A sentry standing guard at the Queen's House saw and challenged a white shape that appeared suddenly veiled in mist. When his challenge went unanswered he put his bayonet into the figure but was overcome by severe shock when it passed right through without meeting any resistance. The sentry's story was corroborated by two onlookers who saw the incident from a window in the Bloody Tower: he was acquitted of dereliction of duty by the court. In later years the same apparition was seen by other guards. It is not known what details convinced the sentry or his officers that the ghost was that of Anne Boleyn – we can only accept that a hundred years of tradition makes it so.

The ghost of Thomas Wentworth, Earl of Strafford, is another that has been identified. His bitter comment 'Put not your trust in Princes for in them is no salvation' sums up his relationship with Charles I, the King who found it expedient to condemn a friend to death to hide his own shortcomings. Strafford died bravely on the scaffold, yet his spirit proved restless, appearing to his old political rival Archbishop Laud, himself a prisoner at the time and with whom he had requested a final meeting. Perhaps because this was denied him, Strafford's ghost visited Laud in his cell, reproved him for his misdemeanours, and told him to have no fear. Later the same night, before Laud had recovered from the shock of Wentworth's visitation, the old man was further disturbed by the sudden appearance of the ghost of Cardinal Wolsey. Perhaps this was a premonition, as Laud was himself executed four years later.

Much of the Tower's reputation as a grim, evil fortress stems from the famous story of the little Princes of the Bloody Tower, murdered by order of their wicked uncle who was later to become Richard III. This happened soon after they had been imprisoned here in 1483: King Edward V was twelve years old and his brother Richard, Duke of York only nine. No one knew their fate for certain until 1674 when two small skeletons were found beneath a stairway outside the White Tower. It was generally assumed that this was where the Princes had been hidden after their murders, and their ghosts are said to have ceased to haunt the Bloody Tower after the bones had been reburied in Westminster Abbey. Certainly there have been no recent reports of a pathetic pair of little-boy ghosts clad in long white nightgowns.

On 24 October 1618 Sir Walter Raleigh was executed at Westminster after enduring thirteen years of imprisonment in the Bloody Tower. His ghost frequents 'Raleigh's Walk' where the old adventurer used to exercise during his long captivity.

Although their ghosts have never been identified, James, Earl of Derwentwater, and Charles Radcliff, his younger brother, have good cause to haunt this place. Their family had a curse of extinction laid that was fulfilled with the death of the two brothers:

When a green oakleaf is turned to red
The last earl shall die in his gory bed.
The fox and the owl shall inhabit his halls,
The bat and the spider shall cling to his walls,
His lands from his house the strong arm shall sever
And the name of his race be extinguished forever.

As they were a Catholic family it was only too easy for this curse to be effective in the seventeenth and eighteenth centuries. James, the last Earl, was persuaded to take up arms against George I in the first Jacobite Rebellion. It is a tradition that he came to his decision riding by the banks of a stream – the Devil's Water – on his estate. Glancing up through the foliage of an oak tree he saw one red leaf prematurely sere amongst a thousand green ones.

Both brothers fought at Preston for the Jacobites and both were captured – James being sent to the Tower of London and imprisoned in the Devereux Tower. He was sentenced to death for insurrection and he lost his title and estates by attainment. Much pressure was brought to bear upon the King to secure the reprieve of this young and popular nobleman. However, when it was learnt that Robert Walpole, one of the chief Ministers, had been offered a bribe of

£60,000 to save him from execution, the sentence was ordered to be carried out and he was beheaded on Tower Hill on 24 February 1716. He was twenty-seven years old.

Meanwhile his younger brother had been imprisoned at Newgate and might have been pardoned but instead of waiting for this he took the chance to escape with thirteen other prisoners. Settling on the Continent and marrying a wealthy widow, he was for a time Secretary to Prince Charles Edward ('Bonnie Prince Charlie'), and made many clandestine trips to England to rally support for the Stuart cause. However in 1745 he was captured off the Dogger Bank, a passenger in a French ship laden with arms for the Jacobite armies. Like his brother he was incarcerated in the Tower and condemned to death under the former sentence. He was allowed one concession: although he was not a member of the peerage (his brother had forfeited the title as part of his punishment) he was allowed death by decapitation rather than by hanging, which would have been his fate otherwise. The sentence was carried out on 8 December 1746.

Thus the curse was fulfilled, as was a gipsy prophecy made to Charles Radcliff in his youth. He was told that all his palm showed was the shape of a bloody axe, its blade turned towards him.

The Martin Tower, at the north-eastern corner of the inner defence-works, has the unenviable reputation of being the haunt of some of the most persistent of the ghosts of the Tower. In the upper rooms there is the phantom of George Boleyn, brother of Anne, who was imprisoned in these chambers before suffering the most hideous form of execution devised by the English system: being hung, drawn and quartered. This was usually reserved for traitors, though others in particular disfavour might also suffer its agonies. The victim was first half-strangled, then cut down and, while still alive, disembowelled, finally the body was cut up into quarters. There were instances of people surviving until the final part of the sentence.

Thomas Percy received a more merciful sentence – he was imprisoned in this tower for sixteen years for his part in the Gunpowder Plot. However his spectre is supposed to be the one that caused the sentries such apprehension during the last century that they would only mount guard in pairs. In the last few years visitors have felt unseen hands attempt to push them down the steep stone steps by the tower.

The Martin Tower was the location of the most famous, and to many the most convincing, of all the supernatural occurrences in the

Tower. This happened during the early years of the last century: it was witnessed by a very credible and distinguished man – Edward Lenthal Swifte, then the Keeper of the Crown Jewels. His position made it impossible for him to tell of his experience at the time, but when he left office he was able to recount it at length in *Notes & Queries* (1860). He wrote:

I have often purposed to leave behind me a faithful record of all that I personally know of this strange story. Forty-three years have passed, and its impression is as vividly before me as on the moment of its occurrence but there are yet survivors who can testify that I have not at any time either amplified or abridged my ghostly experiences.

In 1814 I was appointed Keeper of the Crown Jewels in the Tower, where I resided with my family till my retirement in 1852. One Saturday night in October, 1817, about the 'witching hour', I was at supper with my wife, her sisters, and our little boy, in the sitting-room of the Jewel House, which – then comparatively modernised – is said to have been the 'doleful prison' of Anne Boleyn, and of the ten bishops whom Oliver Cromwell piously accommodated therein.

For an accurate picture of the *locus in quo* my scene is laid, I refer to George Cruikshank's woodcut in p. 384 of Ainsworth's *Tower of London*. The room was – as it still is – irregularly shaped, having three doors and two windows, which last are cut nearly nine feet deep into the outer wall; between these is a chimney-piece, projecting far into the room, and (then) surmounted with a large oil-painting. On the night in question the doors were all closed, heavy and dark cloth curtains were let down over the windows, and the only light in the room was that of two candles on the table; I sat at the foot of the table, my son on my right hand, his mother fronting the chimney-piece, and her sister on the opposite side. I had offered a glass of wine and water to my wife, when, on putting it to her lips, she paused, and exclaimed, 'Good God! what is that?' I looked up, and saw a cylindrical figure, like a glass-tube, seemingly about the thickness of my arm, and hovering between the ceiling and the table; its contents appeared to be a dense fluid, white and pale azure, like to the gathering of a summer-cloud, and incessantly mingling within the cylinder. This lasted about two minutes, when it began slowly to move *before* my sister-in-law;

The illustration from Ainsworth's Tower of London *referred to in the text.* (BRITISH LIBRARY)

then, following the oblong-shape of the table, *before* my son and myself; passing *behind* my wife, it paused for a moment over her right shoulder (observe, there was no mirror opposite to her in which she could there behold it). Instantly she crouched down, and with both hands covering her shoulder, she shrieked out, 'O Christ! It has seized me!' Even now, while writing, I feel the fresh horror of that moment. I caught up my chair, struck at the wainscot behind her, rushed up-stairs to the other children's room, and told the terrified nurse what I had seen. Meanwhile the other domestics had hurried into the parlour, where their mistress recounted to them the scene, even as I was detailing it above stairs.

The marvel of all this is enhanced by the fact that *neither my sister-in-law nor my son beheld this 'appearance'.* When I the next morning related the night's horror to our chaplain, after the service in the Tower church, he asked me, might not *one* person have his natural senses deceived? And if *one*, why might not *two*? My answer was, if *two*, why not two thousand? an argument which would reduce history, secular or sacred, to a fable.

Mr Swifte's story stimulated a bevy of correspondence to *Notes & Queries*. Readers suggested logical explanations for the phenomena, most of which Mr Swifte was able to demolish effectively. Thus when it was alleged that some prankster might have projected images into the room he pointed out that not only did the thick curtains make this impracticable, but if it had been accomplished then all the people present would have seen the illusion. In one of his replies Mr Swifte mentioned a more sinister episode that occurred at the Tower only a few days after his own experience:

One of the night sentries at the Jewel Office, a man who was in perfect health and spirits, and was singing and whistling up to the moment of the occurrence, was alarmed by a figure like a huge bear issuing from under the Jewel Room door. He thrust at it with his bayonet, which stuck in the door, even as my chair had dinted the wainscot; he dropped in a fit, and was carried senseless to the guard-room.

When on the morrow I saw the unfortunate soldier in the main guard-room, his fellow sentinel was also there, and testified to having seen him at his post just before the alarm, awake and alert, and had even spoken to him. I saw the unfortunate man again on the following day, but changed beyond all recognition; in another day or two, the brave and steady soldier, who would have mounted a breach, or led a forlorn hope with unshaken nerves, *died* – at the presence of a shadow.

Confirmation of this story came from another officer stationed at the Tower at this time. This is his account:

Before the burning of the armouries there was a paved yard in front of the Jewel House, from which a gloomy and ghost-like doorway led down a flight of steps to the Mint. Some strange noises were heard in this gloomy corner; and on a dark night at twelve the sentry saw a figure like a bear cross the pavement and disappear down the steps. This so terrified him that he fell, and in a few hours after, having recovered sufficiently to tell the tale, he died. It was fully believed to have arisen from phantasmagoria. . . . The soldier bore a high character for bravery and good conduct. I was then in my thirtieth year, and was present when his body was buried with military honours in the Flemish burial ground, St Catherine's.

George Offor.

Bear-baiting.

Two footnotes may give this story added interest. In his book *Haunted Houses* Charles Harper wrote:

> Whether or not the soldier died from the effects of seeing a genuine apparition, or was merely the victim of a practical joke, was never known; but the guards were doubled immediately after this affair and no more apparitions appeared. It is remarkable, however, to read in the memoirs of Sir John Reresby, a hundred years earlier, how a somewhat similar apparition was observed at York Castle where a piece of paper, fluttering along the ground, was seen to change into a monkey, and then into a bear,* and then to accomplish the amazing feat of squeezing between the door and the doorstep, through a space that would hardly have done more than admit the passage of a coin.

Perhaps it is hardly surprising that the ghost of a bear should haunt the Tower, for these creatures were put to incredible suffering here over the centuries when bear-baiting was a sport. Moreover the Royal Menagerie was housed here from early medieval times until the reign of William IV. Leopards, tigers, lions and elephants were among the animals kept, and it is on record that bears, brown and white, were in captivity. The polar bears were taken on leash to the river to catch their own fish! Another ghostly bear haunts Cheyne Walk, Chelsea.

In 1964 G. W. Lambert put forward the 'vortex' theory to explain the 'glass-tube' seen by Mr Swifte and his family. In Volume 42 of *The Journal for Psychical Research* he wrote:

*Another, earlier account says that it finally turned into a turkey-cock.

In certain conditions, which are not well understood, vortices are set up in the atmosphere. They are only rendered visible (*a*) if they pick up light objects like dust or sand into a sort of column, or (*b*) occur in very humid conditions, with the result that the air in the centre of the vortex, cooler than that surrounding it, precipitates moisture into a visible cloud of roughly columnar shape. Vortices, which have often been observed picking up hay in hayfields in the summer, are seen to move horizontally at about 4 m.p.h., i.e. at about the rate at which a man walks. Thus a misty 'figure', some 5 or 6 feet high, moving at 'walking' speed, may easily be mistaken for a 'ghost'. If it is taller than a man, it is even more terrifying. Vortices are usually encountered out of doors, but there is no obvious reason why small ones should not occasionally form indoors.

Lambert developed his theory to show that there have been stories of unaccountable clouds of mist forming in old castles since the seventeenth century. Further, the primitive methods of sanitation in such a place could bring about sufficient generation of methane gas to give a cold flame effect ('corpse candles', or will o' the wisps). This was particularly likely to occur in a building close to the Thames, which in 1817 was virtually an open sewer.

Tower Hill, the open space in front of the entrance to the Tower, also has its ghosts. During the Second World War a sentry guarding the main gate (the Tower was then used as a prison for spies and turncoats) watched aghast as a stately procession passed his post. Priests and soldiers clad in the dress of a bygone age came first, then a stretcher borne by solemn attendants. On it lay the body of a man, his head rested in the crook of his arm, in the classic manner of ghosts. Not surprisingly the sentry called the guard out, but by the time they arrived the cortège had vanished. The next day the sentry wrote down his account of the incident. His description of the costume enabled experts to identify the uniforms as those worn by the Sheriff of London's men in medieval times. Then, prisoners were taken from the Tower and handed over to the Sheriff for execution on Tower Hill. Afterwards the body was brought back for burial in the churchyard within the precincts of the Tower, while the head was often taken for display on one of the series of spikes erected for the purpose on London Bridge.

The City Churches

All Hallows-by-the-Tower, in Byward Street, suffered badly from bomb damage but was restored by the efforts of the founder of the Toc H movement, 'Tubby' Clayton, who was its vicar. Before the war there were reports of it being haunted by the ghost of a white Persian cat which in its lifetime had been owned by the organist, Miss Liscette Rist. She was a great animal-lover and made it her personal task to sand the road that led from the docks up to Tower Hill so that the horses working there should not slip. Her Persian cat would accompany her to church for services, and when it died she asked that she should be allowed to bury it in consecrated ground. This request was refused, which may account for the cat returning to haunt All Hallows. There are no reports of its having been seen in the restored church.

The Church of St Magnus the Martyr is on Fish Street Hill, close to the Monument and to London Bridge. The previous church on the site was the first to be burnt down in the Great Fire; the present one is by Wren. Its ghost is a monastic figure who wears an old-fashioned cowled robe. He had been seen by many people inside the church and seems to be a gentle sort of spirit, though he did once frighten one good lady of the church by appearing without a head. The ghost is often seen close to the tomb of Miles Coverdale, Bishop of Exeter, who first translated the Bible into English – this gives rise to speculation that it is Coverdale's spirit that haunts the church. A peculiar aura of sadness emanates from the figure, and many people alone in the church have the feeling that they are being secretly watched, a sense generated by lots of old buildings which is very disquieting to some people.

Before the Great Fire the King's Wardrobe – which contained the ceremonial clothing used on State occasions – was situated close to St Andrew's Church, Queen Victoria Street, which thus carried the suffix '-by-the-Wardrobe'. It is a church built by Wren that suffered badly in the Blitz but has been rebuilt and is now the headquarters of the Redundant Churches Fund. In 1937 a bell named Gabriel was hung in its tower. This was cast in Worcester in the mid fifteenth century and had previously been at Avenbury in Herefordshire until the belfry there became unsafe. Gabriel is said always to have rung of his own accord on the death of a Vicar of Avenbury, and one

St Andrew's-by-the-Wardrobe.

authority (Jack Hallam) maintains that he heralded the demise of an Avenbury vicar from the tower of St Andrew's during his brief sojourn there.

Wren's masterpiece – St Paul's Cathedral – has a ghost: he is an elderly clergyman who haunts All Souls' Chapel at the west end of the cathedral, just by the visitors' entrance. The chapel was rededicated after the First World War and is now the Kitchener Memorial Chapel, commemorating not just the Field-Marshal but all who served in the Army and died in that conflict. It is said that when the chapel was redesigned a secret stairway was revealed at the very spot where the ancient cleric would disappear, melting into the stonework. Two accounts say that the stairway led directly to the dome – this is clearly ridiculous since the length of the nave separates the chapel from the crossing. However all the vergers who have seen the ghost mentioned one unusual characteristic – its high-pitched, tuneless, whistle.

From St Paul's let us walk up the steps and pass through the

Paternoster Square development to emerge on Newgate Street. Opposite is a quiet oasis amid the bustle of the City – Greyfriars churchyard, which also has the sparse remains of Christ Church. This was founded by the Franciscans in 1209, and soon became a powerful monastery. Queen Isabella was buried here, with the heart of her husband, whom she had brutally murdered, on her breast. Little wonder that she is supposed to haunt the churchyard. Another murderess to walk here is Lady Alice Hungerford. She was acclaimed as the great beauty of her generation, but poisoned her second husband and was hanged at Tyburn in 1523. On one infamous occasion her ghost met that of Queen Isabella and such was their rivalry that an unholy row broke out among the tombstones. The onlookers fled in terror. The third lady to haunt Greyfriars is Elizabeth Barton, 'the Holy Maid of Kent', a humble serving-girl prone to spectacular fits who was manipulated so that in delirium she seemed to speak against Henry VIII's plan to divorce his first wife in order to marry Anne Boleyn. She was supposed to have prophesied that he would lose his throne should he remarry. In the event Henry survived but the Holy Maid perished, being executed, again at Tyburn, in 1534. She was buried in Greyfriars but never takes sides in the dispute between the other two lady ghosts.

'Stop stranger, stop as you pass by. As you are now, so once was I. As I am now, you soon will be, so pray prepare to follow me.' So read the inscription on the case containing old Jimmy Garlickhythe, the mummified remains of an unknown medieval gentleman which used to be on display in the Church of St James, Garlickhythe, in Upper Thames Street. His ghost became particularly active after a bomb crashed through the roof of this beautiful Wren church in 1942. Miraculously it failed to explode, and ended up harmlessly in the crypt. Old Jimmy did not take kindly to the disturbance, and was seen on several occasions in different parts of the church. No one knows who 'Old Jimmy' was, though it seems certain that he was of considerable importance as he was buried in a coffin made of glass, a great status symbol in the Middle Ages (keeping down with the Jones's, in fact). Perhaps he was one of the six Lord Mayors of London to be buried in this church.

A ghostly cat is also said to have been seen in St James's: it would be more appropriate if this were seen in the neighbouring Church of St Michael Paternoster Royal, in College Hill. This is another Wren church, again restored after bomb damage, where a mummified cat,

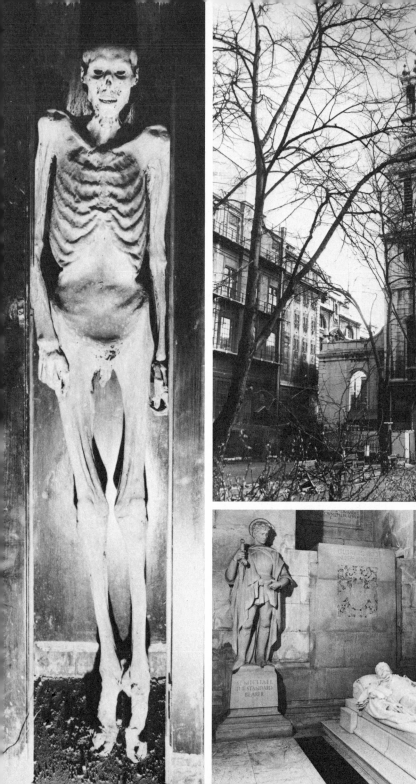

found when the church was rebuilt, is kept in a glass case. This is a highly appropriate trophy for the church, as the original building contained the tomb of Dick Whittington, who died in 1423.

Legend tells how as a young man Richard Whittington came to London from the country to seek his fortune. At first he was unsuccessful and he decided to return home, accompanied by a cat who had, in the ways of those animals, adopted him. When he reached Highgate Hill he paused and heard Bow Bells say: 'Turn again Whittington, thrice Mayor of London.' He obeyed them and with his cat returned to the city where he soon became wealthy and was, in fact, Lord Mayor three times. An inscribed stone surmounted by a cat marks the place on Highgate Hill where he heard the bells.

The massive Norman pillars of the nave give the Church of St Bartholomew-the-Great a completely different atmosphere to that of the Wren churches. Perhaps that is why it is the most haunted of the City churches, or is it because of the awful scenes which took place in front of its beautiful gatehouse, which faces Smithfield?

At a spot known as 'The Elms' many hundreds of people met their deaths, in a variety of hideous ways. A poisoner was boiled alive, and a Prior of Greenwich roasted to death in an iron cage, on the orders of Henry VIII whose authority over the Church he had denied. Most, however, were burned at the stake. If they were fortunate, and the executioner could reach them before the flames grew too fierce, they were strangled first – but many were burnt alive. In the reign of Mary 270 were put to death in this way in England for heresy. Many of them died here in Smithfield, facing east, and the old gateway to the Church of St Bartholomew-the-Great. Small wonder that their ghostly cries still echo through the ether, and these, with the sound of crackling faggots, have been heard by people passing by here alone, on dark nights. Some have even spoken of also smelling the hideous stench of charred flesh.

The ghostly monk said to haunt the church itself is usually taken to be its founder, Rahere, who built the original priory here in 1123, and thus founded the famous hospital as well. He was apparently a minstrel or jester at the Court of Henry I who became a convert to the religious way of life when he was sickened by the frivolity of the Court. While on pilgrimage to Rome he caught malaria and came very close to death. He promised in his prayers to build a hospital for the poor if his life should be spared, and after recovering dreamed that St Bartholomew visited him and directed him to Smithfield,

Left: 'Old Jimmy' Garlickhythe. Right, top: Greyfriars; below: All Souls' Chapel, St Paul's Cathedral (note the shadowy figure in the doorway, the negative has not been tampered with).

69

Wale del.   Grignion sculp.

Manner of BURNING *the* MARTYRS *in* Smithfield

where he was to build the hospice and church.

The Reverend W. F. G. Sandwith was Rector of St Bartholomew's during the early years of this century. He was a man sensitive to ghosts, and saw here not only the monkish figure of Rahere, but another, even more intriguing spectre:

I was taking two ladies round the church, and quite suddenly, looking at the pulpit, I saw in it a man in the black gown of Geneva, evidently a Divine of the Reformation period, preaching away most earnestly to an invisible congregation. No sound was to be heard, but he appeared to be exhorting the unseen audience with the greatest fervour, gesticulating vehemently, bending first to the right, then to the left over the pulpit, thumping the cushions in front of him, and all the while his lips moving as though speech was pouring from them. I looked at him in some dismay because I was afraid that the ladies who were with me might be upset, but as the moments passed and they made no remark about the apparition, I determined to ascertain whether they did, or did not, see it. With this object I pointed straight at the pulpit where the man was preaching and remarked——

'I don't think that pulpit is quite worthy of the church, do you?'

'No, perhaps not,' she replied without further comment, and after a while I turned to her companion and pointed to a monument near the pulpit.

'That is a very interesting old Jacobean effigy there,' I remarked, thus making her, also, look in the direction of the pulpit. She agreed with me, indifferently, in a manner which showed me conclusively that she saw nothing unusual in the direction to which I thus caused her to look. Yet for fully a quarter of an hour I remained in the church seeing that man in the pulpit as clearly as I see you beside me.

(From *Ghosts Vivisected* by A. M. W. Stirling.)

Mrs Stirling also describes a meeting Mr Sandwith's wife had with Rahere:

It seems that on the previous Christmas Eve, Mrs. Sandwith was arranging flowers at the altar in the church when she heard a faint sound behind her, and, looking round, she saw the figure of a monk standing at a little distance. His cowl was drawn over his head and his face was invisible. She spoke to him, but he did not answer, and as she watched him, he glided away noiselessly into the vestry. She at once followed, but to her astonishment found no one there; whereupon she went home and told her husband of her uncanny experience.

'The next day, Christmas Day,' said Mr. Sandwith, continuing his wife's story, 'I was celebrating Holy Communion when I looked up, and, to my astonishment, on the capital of one of the pillars adjacent, apparently looking down at me, was a monk's face encircled by a cowl. I was so amazed that I paused in the middle of the service, and only when I became aware that the congregation were looking at me in surprise, did I continue, while the face above me faded away; but the curious thing was that my wife saw the body of the apparition without the face and I saw the face without the body.'

Rahere has been seen many times since then. He is a tranquil ghost, and his aura sheds a feeling of peace over those he appears to. The Lady Chapel is a location particularly favoured by him, though one elderly lady connected with the church believed that he was always certain to appear in the nave on the first day of July, at seven in the morning.

All hospitals have ghosts, though most of the staff feel that it would be unsettling for the peace of mind of their patients to have them publicised, for so often they appear before death. This does not, however, apply to the Grey Lady of Grace Ward, who is supposed to be the ghost of a nurse killed by a mentally disturbed patient.

A ghostly monk also haunts Charterhouse, once a Carthusian monastery and the original home of the famous school. This was founded by Thomas Sutton in 1611 as a hospital for forty poor boys and men. The boys moved out to Godalming in 1872, but the charity still provides accommodation for a few elderly men here, who have the chance of seeing the headless ghost of Thomas Howard, fourth Duke of Norfolk, descend the staircase of the Great Hall. He was executed for treason in the reign of Elizabeth I.

When the school occupied the building, the square was used as an area for recreation. Some 500 years previously it had been a burial-ground for some of the 500,000 inhabitants of London who died of the Black Death, and boys of the school would dare one another to listen, with ear to the ground at dead of night, for the moans of those mistakenly buried alive long ago.

Newgate

Newgate was the most infamous of London's gaols: its history extends back to Norman times, and it lasted until 1901, when it was demolished to make room for the Central Criminal Court (Old Bailey). The judges there are reminded of the old prison by a curious custom that still survives – at the beginning of each case held in the summer the judge is presented with a nosegay originally intended to mask the aroma emanating from Newgate. Amen Court, where many of the churchmen from St Paul's live, backs on to the site of the old prison and its graveyard, and a particularly horrific ghost crawls along the old wall that originally separated the Court from the prison.

The Black Dog of Newgate is the most venerable of all the ill-famed ghosts here. It must have been known in folklore long before anything was written down: the earliest record of its existence dates from about 1596 and was written by an inmate named Luke Hutton. This version of the story is a diatribe against the evil of his fellow prisoners, and tells of the terrible tricks which have brought them

Amen Court – the shapeless monster would crawl along the ivy-covered wall at the end.

The Blacke Dogge of Newgate:

both pithie and profitable
for all Readers.

Vide, Lege, Caue.

Time shall trie the trueth.
by Luke Hutton

Imprinted at London by G. Simson and W. White.

there. Hutton dedicated his work to the Lord Chief Justice, Sir John Popham, and it may have helped him get his release. Nevertheless he failed to take to the straight and narrow subsequently and in 1598 was hanged in York 'for his robberies and trespasses committed thereabout'. The following is taken from the version of 1638, *The discovery of a London Monster, called, the Blacke Dogg of Newgate.*

This tells of the narrator entering a pub (appropriately 'The Black Dog') where he orders his pint of wine and gets into conversation about the dog with a stranger ('a poore Thin-gut fellow'):

I maintained that I had read an old Chronicle that it was a walking spirit in the likenesse of a blacke Dog, gliding up and down the streets a little before the time of Execution, and in the night whilst the Sessions continued, and his beginning thus.

In the raigne of King *Henry* the third there happened such a famine through England, but especially in London, that many starved for want of food, by which meanes the Prisoners in Newgate eat up one another altue, but commonly those that came newly in, and such as could make but small resistance. Amongst many others cast into this Denne of misery, there was a certaine Scholler brought thither, upon suspition of Conjuring, and that he by Charmes and devilish Whitchcrafts, had done much hurt to the kings subjects, which Scholler, mauger his Devils Furies, Spirits and Goblins, was by the famished prisoners eaten up, and deemed passing good meate. This being done, such an idle conceit possessed the mindes of the poore Prisoners, that they supposed, nightly to see the Scholler in the shape of a black Dog walking up and downe the Prison, ready with his ravening Jawes to teare out their bowels: for his late human flesh they had so hungerly eaten, and withall they hourely heard (as they thought) strange groanes and cries, as if it had been some creature in great paine and torments, whereupon such a nightly feare grew amongst them, that it turned to a Frenzie, and from a Frenzie to Desperation, in which desperation they killed the Keeper, and so many of them escaped forth, but yet whither soever they came or went they imagined a Blacke Dog to follow, and by this means, as I doe thinke, the name of him began.

"Not so" quoth Signior Thin-gut, "I thinke it rather an idle fiction than a probable truth; but this I must tell you Sir, I know it for a truth, that there is no other blacke Dog, that I ever saw or

heard of, but a great blacke stone standing in the dungeon called *Limbo*, the place where the condemned Prisoners be put after their Judgement, upon which they set a burning candle in the night, against which I have heard that a desperate condemned Prisoner dashed out his braines."

Is this 'the black shape' that creeps along the high wall at the end of Amen Court? The shape is never seen definitely enough to say whether it is man or beast, or a nameless, amorphous horror, but over the long centuries of its history Newgate has seen enough evil to have generated not just one ghost, but legions.

Which brings an interesting coincidence to mind – for this particular wall was a part of the original, Roman, boundary wall of London. On the Newgate side of it there was a narrow passage which ran from the prison to the pits where the bodies of those executed were buried in quicklime. This was known as 'Dead Man's Walk', and for much of its length its paving was a cast-iron grating which gave footsteps a distinctive, ringing sound. The last man to be buried in the lime-pit was lame, and the hesitant sound of his feet on the iron sometimes disturbs the night-time peace of the City. However as interest in anatomy increased, fewer bodies reached the pits at the end of Dead Man's Walk. There was eager demand from the hospitals for the corpses of executed felons. *The Diary of a Resurrectionist* tells of the procedure:

The executions generally took place at eight o'clock on Mondays, and the 'cut down,' as it is called, at nine, although there was no cutting at all, as the rope, with a large knot at the end, was simply passed through a thick and strong ring, with a screw, which firmly held the rope in its place, and when all was over, Calcraft, *alias* 'Jack Ketch,' would make his appearance on the scaffold, and by simply turning the screw, the body would fall down. At once it would be placed in one of those large carts with collapsible sides, only to be seen in the neighbourhood of the Docks, and then preceded by the City Marshal in his cocked hat, and, in fact, all his war paint, with Calcraft and his assistant in the cart, the procession would make its way to 33 Hosier Lane, West Smithfield, in the front drawing room of which were assembled Sir William Blizard, President of the Royal College of Surgeons, and members of the Court desirous of being present, with Messrs. Clift (senior and junior), Belfour, and myself. On extraordinary occasions visitors were admitted by special favour. The bodies would then be stripped, and the clothes removed by Calcraft as his valuable perquisites, which, with the fatal rope, were afterwards exhibited to the morbidly curious, at so much per head, at some favoured public-house. It was the duty of the City Marshal to be present to see the body 'anatomised,' as the Act of Parliament had it. A crucial incision in the chest was enough to satisfy the important City functionary above referred to, and he would soon beat a hasty retreat, on his gaily-decked charger, to report the due execution of his duty. These experiments concluded, the body would be stitched up, and Pearson, an old museum attendant, would remove it in a light cart to the hospital, to which it was intended to present it for dissection.

In 1783 the New Prison had been completed at Newgate, and executions took place there rather than at Tyburn. These events were eagerly awaited, and great crowds gathered to see the poor wretches suffer. On 23 February 1807, John Holloway and Owen Haggerty were brought to the scaffold for the murder of a Mr Steele, a lavender-merchant. Both men denied committing the crime to the last: the *Newgate Calendar* tells how they met their fate, and of the dreadful events that followed:

Owen Haggerty first ascended the scaffold. His arms were pinioned, and the halter had been already placed round his neck: he wore a white cap, and a light olive shag great-coat: he looked downwards, and was silent. He was attended by a Roman Catholic clergyman, who read to him, and to whom the unfortunate culprit seemed to pay great attention; he made no public acknowledgement of guilt. After the executioner had tied the fatal noose, he brought up Holloway, who wore a smock frock and jacket, as it had been stated by the approver that he did at the time of the murder: he had also a white cap on, was pinioned, and had a halter round his neck: he had his hat in his hand; and mounting the scaffold, he jumped and made an awkward bow, and said, "I am innocent, innocent, by God!" He then turned round, and, bowing, made use of the same expressions, "Innocent, innocent, innocent! Gentlemen!—No verdict! No verdict! No verdict! Gentlemen. Innocent! Innocent!" At this moment, and while in the act of saying something more, the executioner proceeded to do his office, by placing the cap over his face; to which he, with apparent reluctance, complied; at the same time uttering some words which were not heard. As soon as the rope was fixed round his neck, he continued quiet. He was attended in his devotions by an assistant at Rowland Hill's Chapel.

The last that mounted the scaffold was Elizabeth Godfrey. She had been a woman of the town, aged 34, and had been capitally convicted of the wilful murder of Richard Prince, in Mary-le-bone parish, on the 25th of December 1806, by giving him a mortal wound with a pocket-knife in the left eye, of which wound he languished and died. Immediately on receiving sentence, this woman's firmness and recollection seemed to fail her, and she appeared bordering upon a state of frenzy. At the place of execution she was dressed in white, with a close cap, and long sleeves, and was attended by the Rev. Mr Ford, the Ordinary of Newgate; but her feelings appeared to be much overpowered, that notwithstanding she bore the appearance of resignation in her countenance, her whole frame was so shaken by the terror of her situation, that she was incapable of any actual devotion.

They were all launched off together, at about a quarter after eight. It was a long time before the body of the poor female seemed to have gone through its last suffering.

The crowd which assembled to witness this execution was unparalleled, being, according to the best calculation, near 40,000; and the fatal catastrophe, which happened in consequence, will cause the day long to be remembered. By eight o'clock, not an inch of ground was unoccupied in view of the platform, and the pressure of the crowd was so great, that before the malefactors appeared, numbers of persons were crying out in vain to escape from it. The attempt only tended to increase the confusion, and several females of low stature, who had been so imprudent as to venture among the mob, were in a dismal situation: their cries were dreadful. Some, who could be no longer supported by the men, were suffered to fall, and were trampled to death, and this was also the case with several boys. In all parts there were continual cries of "Murder! murder!"

particularly from the female part of the spectators and children, some of whom were seen expiring without the possibility of obtaining the least assistance, every one being employed in endeavours to preserve his own life. The most affecting scene of distress was seen at Green Arbour lane, nearly opposite the Debtor's-door. The terrible occurrence which took place near this spot was attributed to the circumstance of two pie-men attending there to dispose of their pies, and it appears that one of them having his basket overthrown, which stood upon a sort of stool upon four legs, some of the mob, not being aware of what had happened, and at the same time being severely pressed, fell over the basket and the man, at the moment he was picking it up, together with its contents. Those who fell were never more suffered to rise, and were soon numbered with the dead.

At this fatal place a man of the name of Herrington was thrown down, who had in his hand his youngest son, a fine boy, about twelve years of age. The youth was soon trampled to death; but the father recovered, though much bruised, and was amongst the wounded in St. Bartholomew's Hospital. A woman, who was so imprudent as to bring with her a child at the breast, was one of the number killed: whilst in the act of falling, she forced the child into the arms of the man nearest to her, requesting him, for God's sake, to save its life; but the man, finding it required all his exertions to preserve himself, threw the infant from him. It was fortunately caught at a distance by another man, who, finding it difficult to ensure its safety or his own, got rid of it in a similar way. The child was then again caught by a person, who contrived to struggle with it to a cart, under which he deposited it until the danger was over, and the mob was dispersed.

In other parts, the pressure was so great that a horrible sense of confusion ensued, and seven persons lost their lives by suffocation alone. A cart which was overloaded with spectators broke down, and some of the persons falling from the vehicle, were trampled under foot and never recovered.

During the hour for which the malefactors hung, little assistance could be afforded to the unhappy sufferers; but after the bodies were cut down, and the gallows removed to the Old Bailey yard, the marshals and constables cleared the street, and then, shocking to relate, there lay near one hundred persons dead, or in a state of insensibility, strewed round the street. Twenty-seven dead bodies were taken to St. Bartholomew's Hospital; four to St. Sepulchre's church; one to the Swan on Snow-hill, one to a public-house opposite St. Andrew's church, Holborn; one, an apprentice to his master's, Mr. Broadwood, pianoforte maker, Golden-square; a mother was seen carrying away the body of her dead boy; and the body of Mr. Harrison, a respectable gentleman, was taken to his house at Holloway. There was a sailor-boy killed opposite Newgate by suffocation: he carried a small bag, in which he had some bread and cheese, from which it was concluded that he had come some distance to witness the execution.

The fate of Mary Green, who came to the scaffold at Newgate in 1819, had a happier outcome:

MARY GREEN, WHO AFTER BEING HUNG CAME TO LIFE AGAIN.

This young woman, being left an orphan at three years of age, was brought up in a respectable family till her fifteenth year, when she was placed in service, where she continued till her marriage in 1810. Her husband treated her badly, but for eight years she bore it uncomplainingly, when he suddenly left her altogether and totally destitute. She followed him to Battle Bridge, where he was at work, but he refused her any aid. At this time, and thus situated, she fell into the company of a set of forgers of bank notes, but though earnestly entreated to become one in passing them, she steadily refused. At length stern necessity left her no other resource; she yielded, was arrested, tried, convicted, and sentenced to expiate such a crime (which was more justly her husband's than her own) on the scaffold. Exertions were made to save her, but they all failed, and this unhappy woman was doomed to undergo her sentence. She was executed at Newgate on March 22nd, 1819, and after hanging the usual time, was cut down and her body delivered to her friends. When preparing for her burial, they were startled by finding signs of returning life. Dr Beddell was sent for, and in twenty minutes she perfectly recovered. God had more mercy on her than her judges, and thus showed His mercy in restoring her to life. What her wretched husband's feelings must have been on hearing of her execution, is known only to his Maker. Thus singularly released from her husband, she lived under a feigned name, in the neighbourhood of Old St. Pancras, as a reputable and thrifty woman, and on her decease, many years afterwards, was buried in the old graveyard. (*History of St Pancras.*)

Thurston Hopkins, a writer about the supernatural working about fifty years ago, told a chilling story of Newgate in his book *Ghosts over England*. He became friendly with the Chief Warder of Newgate, Mr Scott, who attended the execution of Mrs Amelia Dyer, the Reading baby-farmer, on 10 June 1896. Paid handsomely to look after unwanted babies, she saved herself the expense by drowning them in the Thames and other rivers. Mrs Dyer was a well-behaved prisoner, yet she had a way of looking at Mr Scott which made him acutely uncomfortable. Her small, evil eyes, which belied the greasy smile on her face, brought a chill to his soul. As she passed him on the way to the scaffold, she paused, and said to him quietly, 'I'll meet you again, some day, sir.' Hopkins described the sequel to this:

One night just before Newgate was closed down for good several of the warders were having a bottle of whisky together to celebrate the final week of duty in the prison. They were sitting in the Keeper's room next to the Women Felons Yard. There was a door with a glass observation wicket looking out to the yard. Suddenly Scott felt aware that someone's eyes were fixed on him, and he heard a voice ringing in his head: 'Meet you again . . . meet you again some day, sir.' . . . Then he looked towards the door and Mrs. Dyer's face was framed in the grille. There was no mistaking her oily benevolent smile, the little dark, snake-like eyes and the thin lips trying to look kind and harmless. She gave Scott one sad enigmatical look and passed on. Scott jumped up and opened the door and saw nothing except a woman's handkerchief which fluttered at his feet on the wet flagstones.

There was no woman convict in the prison at that time – indeed the reception of women prisoners had been discontinued for some years.

Later in the same book Thurston Hopkins describes how when Chief Warder Scott was photographed outside the execution shed, Mrs Dyer's face appeared behind his shoulder on the print.

Elliott O'Donnell, in his book on London ghosts, tells how the night before demolition was due to commence the watchman and his wife were in the kitchen having supper when the bell in the condemned cell began to ring. The watchman hurried to investigate, only to find no one there but the bell still gently swinging. . . .

82   *Chief Warder Scott and the Medical Officer of Newgate pose beneath the grating which gave Birdcage Walk its name. The bodies of executed prisoners were buried in quicklime beneath the flagstones.*
(GUILDHALL LIBRARY)

The Cock Lane Uproar

Sold by C Dicey & Co. in Aldermary Church Yard.

At Miss Fanny's New Theatre in Cock Lane
By particular Desire of Several Persons of Distinction
This Evening will be performed *The Old Which* by Miss ...... J R ......
An Entertainment Entitan No Pastery of two dogs *The Mouse*
to Conclude with a Scatter of singing and whistling by a Gentleman
Be dam 6 Chairs .... s 0
to begin precisely, at 12 o'Clock
Principal parts to be performed are
first by Miss P 3

Standing s........ 0
The Knocker or Token, the by Un old Gentleman
to be retired by M. P ....
The Prompter by M. P 3

Flatterers Interpreters Kidneys Rafus & Company

The Cock Lane Ghost

Cock Lane is a narrow thoroughfare that leads off Giltspur Street opposite St Bartholomew's Hospital. In 1762, the year it became famous for its ghost, Cock Lane was a seedy street of tenements with tradespeople occupying the ground floor of many of the properties.

One such house was the home of William Parsons, a Verger at St Sepulchre's, Holborn. He had met a well-to-do Norfolk gentleman, William Kent, at the church, and when their conversation gave him to understand that Kent was looking for rooms in the City, he was able to offer him accommodation in his own house. Kent was a widower and was living with his late wife's sister, whom he was forbidden to marry by the laws of the Church, much to their mutual regret. At first the arrangement worked well, but Parsons borrowed money from his lodger which he proved reluctant to repay: naturally this led to ill-feeling which was at its height when Kent was called away to a family gathering in Norfolk, leaving his common-law wife, 'Miss Fanny', in the care of the Parsons family. She was a nervous lady, and because of this persuaded the Parsons' eleven-year-old daughter, Elizabeth, to sleep with her. This was the start of the disturbances – both Miss Fanny and the child were kept awake by extraordinary noises, which at first they attributed to a neighbouring cobbler. However this proved not to be the case as they continued unabated, even on the Lord's Day, causing Miss Fanny considerable disquiet, as she had begun to believe that they foretold her death. On his return Kent took his 'wife' away from the house to new lodgings in Clerkenwell. In the meantime the noises went on in the Parsons' house, disturbing the elder daughter and her sister in their bedroom, but not the rest of the household. Mr Kent began the process of suing Parsons for the money that was owed him.

By January of the following year Miss Fanny was dead. Officially the cause of death was given as smallpox, but events in the Parsons' house in Cock Lane soon threw suspicion on this. Firstly the scratching and knocking was resumed with renewed vigour, and the elder of the daughters actually saw the ghost, and identified it as Miss Fanny. She had appeared in her shroud, without hands, 'all luminous and shining'.

By now the ghost had achieved considerable local notoriety, and many visitors came to the house to hear the strange noises that it produced. A 'one tap yes, two taps no' means of communicating with the spirit was devised, and by means of this it was found that the spirit was indeed that of Miss Fanny, who believed that she had been poisoned by a glass of purl (a mixture of hot beer and gin) which contained red arsenic.

When news of this got abroad everyone flocked to Cock Lane. Horace Walpole visited the house with the Duke of York:

Even Horace Walpole was magnetically drawn to the clerk's house in Cock Lane. The clever fribble writes to Sir Horace Mann, January 29, 1762: 'I am ashamed to tell you that we are again dipped into an egregious scene of folly. The reigning fashion is a ghost – a ghost, that would not pass muster in the paltriest convent in the Apennines. It only knocks and scratches; does not pretend to appear or to speak. The clergy give it their benediction; and all the world, whether believers or infidels, go to hear it. I, in which number you may guess, go to-morrow; for it is as much the mode to visit the ghost as the Prince of Mecklenburg, who is just arrived. I have not seen him yet, though I have left my name for him.'

Again Walpole writes: – 'I went to hear it, for it is not an apparition, but an audition. We set out from the opera, changed our clothes at Northumberland House, the Duke of York, Lady Northumberland, Lady Mary Coke, Lord Hertford, and I, all in one hackney-coach, and drove to the spot. It rained torrents; yet the lane was full of mob, and the house so full we could not get in. At last they discovered it was the Duke of York, and the company squeezed themselves into one another's pockets to make room for us. The house, which is borrowed, and to which the ghost has adjourned, is wretchedly small and miserable. When we opened the chamber, in which were fifty people, with no light, but one tallow candle at the end, we tumbled over the bed of the child to whom the ghost comes, and whom they are murdering by inches in such insufferable heat and stench. At the top of the room are ropes to dry clothes. I asked if we were to have rope-dancing between the acts. We heard nothing. They told us (as they would at a puppet-show) that it would not come that night till seven in the morning, that is, when there are only 'prentices and old women. We stayed, however, till half an hour after one. The Methodists have promised them contributions. Provisions are sent in like forage, and all the taverns and ale-houses in the neighbourhood make fortunes.'

(Walpole to George Montagu, Feb. 2nd, 1762.)

Already there were many who were suspicious about the authenticity of the ghost, and to allay them Elizabeth was moved to another house (with better accommodation for visitors). The scratching and knocking continued, attracting all the celebrities of the day to the house. A sceptical pamphleteer wrote:

To have a proper idea of this scene, as it is now carried on, the reader is to conceive a very small room, with a bed in the middle; the girl at the usual hour of going to bed, is undressed, and put in with proper solemnity. The spectators are next introduced, who sit looking at each other, suppressing laughter, and wait in silent expectation for the opening of the scene. As the ghost is a good deal offended at incredulity, the persons present are to conceal theirs, if they have any, as by this concealment they can only hope to gratify their curiosity; for, if they show, either before or when the knocking is begun, a too prying, inquisitive, or ludicrous turn of thinking, the ghost continues usually silent, or, to use the expression of the house, 'Miss Fanny is angry.' The spectators, therefore, have nothing for it but to sit quiet and credulous, otherwise they must hear no ghost, which is no small disappointment to persons who have come for no other purpose.

The girl, who knows, by some secret, when the ghost is to appear, sometimes apprizes the assistants of its intended visitation. It first begins to scratch, and then to answer questions, giving two knocks for a negative, but one for an affirmative. By this means it tells whether a watch, when held up, be white, blue, yellow, or black; how many clergymen are in the room, though in this sometimes mistaken. . . . It is sometimes mistaken in questions of a private nature, when it deigns to answer them. For instance, the ghost was ignorant where she had dined upon Mr. K—'s marriage; how many of her relations were at church upon the same occasion; but, particularly, she called her father John, instead of Thomas – a mistake, indeed, a little extraordinary in a ghost. But perhaps she was willing to verify the old proverb, that 'It is a wise child that knows its own father.' However, though sometimes right, and sometimes wrong, she pretty invariably persists in one story, namely, that she was poisoned, in a cup of purl, by red arsenic, a poison unheard of before, by Mr. K—, in her last illness, and that she heartily wished him hanged.

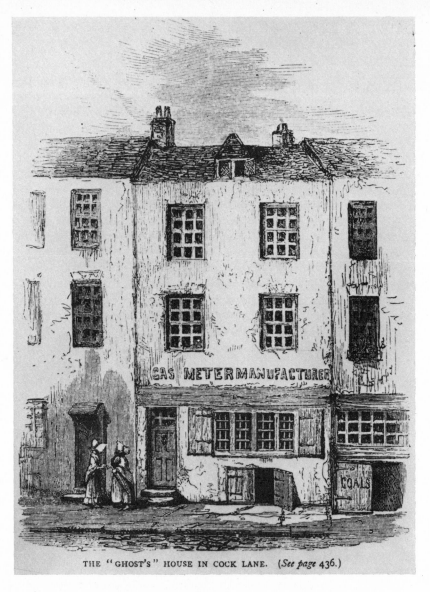

THE "GHOST'S" HOUSE IN COCK LANE. (*See page* 436.)

It is no easy matter to remark upon an evidence of this nature; but it may not be unnecessary to observe, that the ghost, though fond of company, is particularly modest upon these occasions, an enemy to the light of a candle, and always most silent before those from whose rank and understanding she could most reasonably expect redress.

However in the end the ghost became too ambitious and brought about its own downfall. It promised that if certain learned gentlemen would enter the vaults of St John's, Clerkenwell, she would prove her ghostly presence there by knocking three times on the lid of her coffin. A distinguished company accordingly gathered at St John's at the appointed hour, one o'clock in the morning. Dr Johnson was one of them. But when the ghost was called upon to prove itself there was no response. Its fall from grace was complete when subsequent tests were undertaken. With the girl's hands and feet bound no noises were heard. She was threatened with imprisonment in Newgate and not surprisingly she broke down and confessed. A small sounding-board was found concealed in her stays.

Many of the perpetrators of the hoax were prosecuted, and Kent was compensated for the damage done to his character. Yet public sympathy remained with Parsons, and little harm befell him when he was pilloried for three days (perhaps because of the prosperity that the haunting had brought to the area). He was also sentenced to two years in prison. Elizabeth was thought an unwilling accomplice, and did not have to face trial. She was subsequently twice married and died in Chiswick in 1806. An interesting postscript is printed in Walford's *Old and New London*:

"While drawing the crypt of St John's, Clerkenwell," says Mr. J. W. Archer, "in a narrow cloister on the north side, there being at the time coffins, fragments of shrouds, and human remains lying about in disorder, the sexton's boy pointed to one of the coffins, and said that it was 'Scratching Fanny.' This reminding me of the Cock Lane Ghost, I removed the lid of the coffin, which was loose, and saw the body of a woman, which had become adipocere.* The face was perfect, handsome, oval, with an aquiline nose. Will not arsenic produce adipocere? She is said to have been poisoned, although the charge is understood to have been disproved. I inquired of one of the churchwardens of the time, Mr. Bird, who said the coffin had always been understood to contain the body of the woman whose spirit was said to have haunted the house in Cock Lane."

In 1893, 325 coffins were removed from the vaults at St John's; one, unidentifiable, was unmistakably stained with arsenic. . . .

Adipocere: fatty, waxy substance generated in dead bodies buried in moist places.

"Hackney Coachman."

From Fleet Street to Aldgate

Considering how many strange stories have been concocted there in the past, it would seem strange to leave Fleet Street out of this book for want of a ghost, yet only an incident dating from 1684 saves 'the Street of Shame' from neglect. This is the story of the misfortune of Thomas Cox, who on the night of 31 October (is this a significant date?) drove his Hackney carriage up Water Lane, off Fleet Street, and dropped his passenger there. He continued to the bottom of the lane in order to turn the carriage round, and then called in at a pub 'for a pot or two' before gently driving up the lane again. When he was within three or four doors of Fleet Street at the top, he was stopped by the dark figure of a gentleman who appeared to hold a roll of paper or parchment in his hand. Cox was told to drive to Lower Church Yard, by St Bride's Church, and he immediately climbed up on his box and lashed his horses to get them to start. But for some reason they became so difficult to control that he was eventually forced to get down, thoroughly frightened by their unnatural behaviour. Even with the coachman at their heads the horses remained excited and dangerous, lashing out with their hooves. Cox shouted to his passenger to get down, as he could go no further, and the man alighted, and held out his hand towards Cox:

... which the Coach man saw, but no money in it; but when he went to take it could feel no hand, though he saw the same shape of the Gentlemans person in the Coach as before, who presently stept out, at which the Horses started and flying out drew the Coach man back, who having stopped his Horses and looking back to his fare, he saw a great black thing in the form of a Bear with great flaming Eyes which lay by the Wall side and made up to him, at which the Horses press'd forward, and the Coach man with much ado stop'd them, and taking the Reins from his Whip into his Hand, as it approached him whip't at it, and as he thought lash'd it; when on a sudden it vanished away in a terrible flash of Fire with great sparks, as if a Flambeaux had been dashed against the Wall and all flashed in his face, that he was so stoun'd that he did not know where he was, and lost all Sense in the Horrour and Consternation he was in.

(The True Relation of the Devils Appearing to Thomas Cox, a Hackney-Coach-Man.)

Cox was fortunate that the Devil offered him no money, for had he taken any his soul would have been claimed and he would have suffered eternal damnation. As it was, he managed somehow to return to his stables, where he was found speechless, and remained so until the following day, when he was able to tell his story to several divines who seemed to have accepted it as authentic. However his limbs remained benumbed, without sense or feeling, and 'not sensible of any heat though fire is applied to them which you may burn his flesh withall, without making him sensible of any pain or anguish; and it is very much fear'd by his friends that he will never recover the use of them again, but remain in that sad condition as long as he lives.'

As a reproach to those who might say he was drunk, the writer of the above pamphlet was at pains to stress that Cox was 'as free from being fudled as ever he was in his life', yet there is such a tongue-in-cheek quality about the telling of the story that it would convince only the most gullible, even if Cox's encounter had taken place on another night, and not at Hallowe'en.

No. 186 Fleet Street was the address of Sweeney Todd, 'The Demon Barber of Fleet Street'. The famous story tells how the barber's shop

'Easy shaving' – an illustration by Phiz for Martin Chuzzlewit.

Sweeney Todd's premises in Fleet Street in 1832. (GUILDHALL LIBRARY)

had a special chair with a tilting mechanism so that the occupant (usually a customer chosen as probably being 'up from the country', and therefore with no one likely to miss him for a week or so) could be shot neatly straight into the cellar below. If he were unfortunate enough to survive the fall, then Todd would be there almost immediately to finish the job off with his razor. The story spoke of an old underground passage that led from his cellar, below St Dunstan's Church, to another cellar in Bell Yard, part of the premises of Mrs Lovett, a pastrycook. She was Todd's accomplice, and her pies were acclaimed as the best in London by her customers, many of whom worked in the Courts of Justice on the other side of Bell Yard. Of course Todd's victims ended up in Mrs Lovett's pies.

The story made a wonderful melodrama but there is no supporting evidence to show that Sweeney Todd ever existed. Such a villain would have made a great stir when brought to book, and there are no newspaper accounts of his capture or trial. His origins may have derived from a terrible Scottish outlaw named Sawney Bean, who, with an ever-increasing family, terrorised Galloway in the fifteenth century. They set upon travellers, robbed and murdered them, and then cut up the bodies and pickled them in barrels. This is said to have been their only sustenance, and over the years the family interbred with such success that they became a fierce clan menacing the order of the whole district. Innkeepers were arbitrarily executed because vanished travellers had last been seen using their hostelries, and many innocent wayfarers were lynched in the belief that they were members of the gang. In the end, after twenty-five years of butchery, Sawney and his family found the fate they had deserved for so long. Their downfall is described in John Nicholson's *Historical and Traditional Tales connected with the South of Scotland* (1843):

A man and his wife behind him on the same horse, coming one evening home from a fair, and falling into the ambuscade of these merciless wretches, they fell upon them in a furious manner. The man to save himself as well as he could, fought very bravely against them with sword and pistol, riding some of them down by main force of his horse.

In the conflict the poor woman fell from behind him, and was instantly butchered before her husband's face, for the female cannibals cut her throat, and fell to sucking her blood with as great a gusto as if it had been wine: this done, they ript up her belly, and pulled out her entrails. Such a dreadful spectacle made the man make the more obstinate resistance, as he expected the same fate, if he fell into their hands.

It pleased Providence while he was engaged that twenty or thirty who had been at the same fair, came together in a body; upon which Sawney Bean and his bloodthirsty clan withdrew and made the best of their way through a thick wood to their den.

This man, who was the first who had ever fallen in their way, and came off alive, told the whole company what had happened, and showed them the horrid spectacle of his wife, whom the murderers had dragged to some distance, but had not time to carry her entirely off. They were all struck with stupefaction and amazement at what he related: they took him with them to Glasgow, and told the affair to the magistrates of that city, who immediately sent to the King concerning it.

The result of this was that a force of about 400 men were sent to the area who hunted Sawney and his people down ruthlessly. When the men of the gang were captured their legs and hands were cut off and they were left to bleed to death, their womenfolk being compelled to watch the spectacle. When the last of the men expired it became the turn of the women and children, who were all burnt alive in three separate fires. None, it is said, showed any sign of penitence, but cursed their captors to the last.

From this edifying detour to the south of Scotland, we return to the City of London, and an equally ghoulish account from Houndsditch:

The Divils cruelty to Mankind.
BEING

A true Relation of the Life and Death of *George Gibbs*, a *Sawyer* by his Trade, who being many times tempted by the *Devill* to destroy himselfe, did on *Friday* being the 7 of *March* 1663. Most cruelly Ripp up his own Belly, and pull'd out his Bowells and Guts, and cut them in pieces: to the Amazement of all the Beholders, the sorrow of his Friends, and the great grief of his Wife, being not long married: and both young People.

If the synopsis of the ballad (by Charles Hammond) is amusing, the verses themselves prove to be horrifically hilarious:

At twelve a clock at night he rose,
   his Wife being then a bed,
And down to ease himself he goes,
   thus to his Wife he said,
His Wife perswaded him to stay,
   but he was fully bent,
The Divill prompting him on's way,
   and out he present went.

When he came there he shut the door,
   and out his Penknife slip't,
His Belly with it Cut and tore,
   and out his Bowells rip't,
His careful Wife did present rise,
   but when she did come there,
And did behold it with her eyes,
   she trembled with such fear.

Few words she spoke to him but went
   and in some Neighbors brought,
Thinking the worst for to prevent,
   and save his life they thought.
Whilst she was gone he made the Door
   fast to himself within,
But they did break and down it tore,
   and suddenly got in.

His Belly he had rip't up quite,
   and out his Bowels tore,
That such a Devillish bloody sight,
   scarce shown by man before,
The Divill did do it to be sure,
   elce he could nere proceed,
His strength and heart could nere endure,
   to do that cruell deed.

Some of his Gutts were cut in two,
   and mangled in such sort,
That he himself could never doe,
   but had some helper for't.
Eight hours or more this man did live,
   in grievous woe and pain,
What Sustinance they did him give,
   came straight way forth again.

The Divil he said did tempt him long,
   and many times before,
For all he did resist him strong,
   he nere would give him ore,
Thus have you heard the doleful end,
   of *Gibbs*, which is too true,
And take this councill from a Friend,
   for fear you after rue.

Pamphlets and ballads of the seventeenth and eighteenth centuries are a much more profitable source of ghosts for this area than more modern newspapers, etc., probably because so many more people actually lived in the City in those days. An account of poltergeist activity in a house at Puddle-dock is in the Guildhall Library and is dated 1674:

News from

PUDDLE-DOCK

IN

LONDON

OR,

**A Perfect particuler of the strange
Apparitions and Transactions that
have happened in the House of
Mr. EDWARD PITTS next Door to
the STILL at PUDDLE-DOCK**

The House of Mr. *Edward Pitts* at *Puddledock* hath in a very strange and stupendious manner been disturbed these 15 or 16 Nights last past: The House is two Rooms of a Floor; and the two Rooms up one pair of stairs have been for these 15 or 16 Nights between 12 and 1 of the Clock continually haunted. When *Mr. Pitts'* Family are gone, or going to Bed, he looks to see those two doors fast; but in the morning he hath always found them open, except once, which was the last week, and then after he had fastened both those doors, he takes a rope and fastens it to the handle of the door, and from thence to a nail on the stairs; that Night he found that door as he left it, but the other wide open; not one night in all this time but his Goods in these Rooms (the one his Kitchin, the other his Parler) have been removed from one place to another in a most strange manner; In the Kitchin the Pewter hath been taken off the shelves and laid any where about the Room. A Box of Candles of 5 or 6 pound have been taken out of the Box and planted about the Room, some put in Candlesticks, and others laid by two and two, the ends laid contrary ways; but that which is the most remarkable is this, on the last Lords-day at Night, *March* 15. 1674. when this Mr. *Pitts* and his Family were going to Supper, a

Fold-up Table (which stood on one side of the Kitchin) was brought to the fire side; upon which the Meat was set, *Mr. Pitts* takes the Loaf off the Dresser to cut bread to lay on the Table, as he was cutting the Bread he spied upon the Dresser a great thing like a Catt, at which being a little affrighted, he started back Presently calling to his Wife, saying, here's a Catt, I never saw a Catt in this house before, upon which, this Cat-like thing seemed to slide off the Dresser, giving a thump on the Boards, and so vanished away. All *Mr. Pitt*'s Family then in the Room, but none could perceive this strange Catt but only his Daughter of about 15 years of Age, and himself; and they say it was as bigg as any Mastiff Dog; but they could not perceive that it had any Leggs.

The pamphlet goes on to describe other strange incidents that befell the household. In the middle of the night the Watchman reprimanded Mr Pitts for keeping a light burning in the house, though the latter was certain that he had been careful to put out all the lamps and candles before retiring (of course in 1674 fire precautions were very strict). Although he knew that he had to get up to investigate the strange light he found himself utterly unable to do so; at the same time he was conscious of the great light in the bedchamber diminishing little by little until the whole room was dark

... then of a sudden he had as much Light as if it had been clear day. In the morning when it was day he got up and went (as every morning he had been used to do) to see what alterations he could find in his 2 haunted Rooms, when he came down he found his Kitchin-door wide open, as it use to be, but his Parler door was off the Latch a little ajar, barricadoed with a great 2 handed Chair, he thrust the Chair aside and opened the door; when he came into the Room, upon the Table there he found a great Wooden Sand-box, upon which was 2 snuffs of Candles burnt to Ashes, a 3d. Candle had been upon that Box, but that had burnt all one side of the Box, and made such a stink in the house (which I should have mentioned before) that the Woman of the house admired what was Burning that should cause such a stink. This Sand-box Candlestick Mr. Pitts had never seen before, nor had ever been master of such a one in his Life; but that which was yet more Wonderful is this, by this Sand-box was placed upon the Table two Splinters of Wood cross ways, exactly like the form here following.

Three Ends or Corners of this Cross was cleft, and in each cleft there was stuck a Paper printed on both sides as you have here *verbatim.*

Right against this Cross and Papers by the Table was placed a Chair, as if some one had sat there viewing them over.

This night, *March* 16 Mr. *Pitts* intends to have some people to sit up, that may speak to any thing that shall appear, and to demand in the name of the Father, *what are you?*

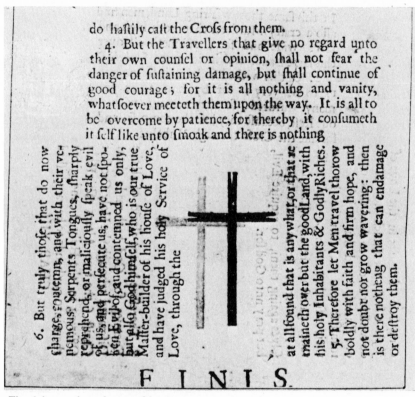

do haftily caft the Crofs from them.

4. But the Travellers that give no regard unto their own counfel or opinion, fhall not fear the danger of fuftaining damage, but fhall continue of good courage; for it is all nothing and vanity, whatfoever meeteth them upon the way. It is all to be overcome by patience, for thereby it confumeth it felf like unto fmoak and there is nothing

F I N I S.

The cleft cross from the pamphlet. (GUILDHALL LIBRARY)

Although there must be some suspicion about the authenticity of the account, there are many features of the haunting that ring true, being typical of poltergeist activity; but one cannot help feeling that the printer had most enjoyment out of this, choosing relevant blocks of type from his old chases with his tongue in cheek.

In 1647 there was a great stir in Lombard Street when the yard of a Mr Youngs was haunted by a very curious ghost. Not only were its pranks troublesome, but it sent divines and other learned men who came to investigate into 'distracted extasy' so that they were able to neither speak or stand. Certainly it was a formidable ghost, able to slam shut a casement window injudiciously opened by a spectator on the third floor of the house that overlooked the yard. The ghost usually disappeared in a spectacular manner, too:

> . . . this hideous MONSTER . . . usually vanishes away, (to the thinking of the beholders) into the ground, then immediately ensueth a noise like to claps of thunder and flashes of fire like lightning seemes to ascend out of the Earthe, and after that a stinking mist, and a noysome sulferous smoake.

An even more harmful ghost was described in *Mercurius Democritus*, a Commonwealth news-book, in February 1654. It walked 'every night among the Butchers at *Smithfield Barrs*, the *Shambles*, *White-chappell* and *Eastcheap*, in the habit of Mallet'.

This probably referred to Sir Thomas Mallet, a Royalist Judge hated by the supporters of Parliament. He had been imprisoned in the Tower but was released in 1644 in an exchange of prisoners. For the remainder of the Commonwealth he was disabled 'as if dead' from being a judge, on the ground of being 'the fomenter and protector of the malignant factor'. At the Restoration he returned to the Bench, but by this time he was seventy-eight years of age, and it was soon discovered that he was too old to serve efficiently. Mallet was given a handsome pension and spent his last years at his country estate.

Since he was still alive at the time of the haunting, it could not be claimed that his ghost was responsible for the chaos it caused: it was sufficient propaganda to say that the ghost looked like him. It passed through the butchers' stalls like a whirlwind, scattering their tables and dislodging carcasses from their hooks. In fury the butchers would slash at the spectral form with cleavers and knives, but the blades always passed through it without doing any harm. However the ghost could be malevolent as well as mischievous: on one occasion he pursued a fair maid, and when he caught her, ate her alive!

Several books on the supernatural were written in the nineteenth century by H. Welby. This extract is from *Signs before Death* (1875):

A shoemaker's wife in the parish of Cripplegate, being thought

Sir Thomas Mallet by an unknown artist. (NATIONAL PORTRAIT GALLERY)

dead, was, agreeable to his desire, buried in her wedding cloaths; her ring being on her finger, induced the sexton to open the grave in the night, in order to steal it: when finding it not easy to come off, he took his knife to cut the finger from the hand; which operation recalled the woman to her senses, and she rose from her coffin. The affrighted villain took to his heels: and she, taking his lanthorn, walked home, knocked up her husband, and lived several years after. Her monument is yet standing in Cripplegate-church.

Remarkably, 250 years before, another H. Welby was living in Cripplegate in a curious style. He was a wealthy gentleman, happily married, with a daughter engaged to be married to a baronet. For some reason he fell out with his younger brother, who fired at him with a pistol. Even though the shot missed, the incident changed Henry Welby's life completely. He shut himself up in three rooms of a house in Grub Street, off Cripplegate, and became a recluse, being attended only by an old maid. He lived the life of a hermit for forty-four years, his only solace being his books, and died in 1640 at the age of eighty-four. He had lived on a diet of gruel, with an occasional salad of herbs, and, even more rarely, the yolk of an egg on feast days. His housekeeper died six days before him.

Returning to the proper subject of this book from these curious detours, the building at the very hub of the City is haunted. This is the Bank of England, whose site covers four acres. The Bank moved to its present position from the old Grocers' Hall in 1734. At the heart of the building is a small enclosed garden haunted by the ghost of Sarah Whitehead since the 1840s.

The Dividend Pay Office at the Bank of England. (GUILDHALL LIBRARY)

Miss Whitehead. insane. she daily attended the Bank of England.

She was the sister of Philip Whitehead, a young bank employee who was arrested in 1811 for forgery. Sarah was devoted to him, and when he was hanged for his crime her mind refused to accept his fate. Instead she used to visit the Bank each day to inquire if her brother had been seen there. Politely they would reply that he had not been in yet that day, and so she would wait for him outside – a sad figure dressed in black, her face garishly rouged.* This was the routine she followed for more than twenty-five years until her death. She is supposed to have been buried in the churchyard of St Christopher-le-Stocks, which was within the environs of the Bank, and later became the garden where she was frequently seen as a sad ghost, still looking for her missing brother.

The ghost of a giant also haunts the Bank. In the days of the 'resurrectionists' one of the cashiers was a man of enormous stature, being nearly eight feet tall. He had an awful dread of his body being disinterred after death by grave-robbers and so persuaded the Governors of the Bank to allow his body to be buried within its precincts. His ghost often terrified members of the Bank picquet, frequently shaking their rifles. Sadly, there are no reports of the electronic surveillance equipment, which took over the Guardsmen's duties in 1973, having ever picked up the echo of his (or Sarah's) ghost, but during excavation work an eighteenth-century lead coffin was discovered. It was seven feet eight inches long, and had an iron chain bound round it.

The Bank Station is believed by London Transport staff to be haunted. Most of the maintenance personnel dislike working there at night because of the strange feeling of despondency and dread which can overcome them. This is accompanied by a smell described as being like that of a newly opened grave.

More 'tangible' is the ghost of Aldgate Station: an old woman who was once seen stroking the hair of an electrician working on the track. Within minutes he had made a mistake which should have been fatal, sending 22,000 volts through his body. Yet though he was knocked out he suffered no other ill-effects, neither did he see or feel the ghost.

*Eric Maple tells of a different motive for her vigil at the Bank. In *Supernatural England* he says that she believed that she was owed a vast fortune, including the whole of the Muswell Hill estate. 'On one occasion she approached Baron Rothschild on the steps of the Stock Exchange and accused him of defrauding her of her fortune. Tactfully Rothschild presented her with a half-crown on account and she cheerfully proceeded on her way.'

The Bethnal Green Ghost

The haunting of 132 Teesdale Street was, literally, a nine-day wonder in February 1938. Although at the end of the affair the ghost was discredited, many aspects of the case remain a mystery, and it may well be that a supernatural occurrence triggered off hysteria which eventually infected two households.

The house in Bethnal Green (which is now demolished) was a three-storey 'workers' dwelling' built in early Victorian times. In the winter of 1937–8 its tenants were the Davis family, headed by sixty-one-year-old Mr George Davis whose wife had died the previous September. She had been born in the house, as had her father, and had brought up a large family there. This consisted of four sons (Albert, Walter, Charles and Sydney, only the latter living at home) and three daughters (Minnie, Nellie and Gracie). The youngest of the daughters, Gracie, was twenty and looked after her father and the young Sydney. Both Minnie and Nellie had married and moved away, though the latter was a frequent visitor to the house with her husband, Alfred Rose, a policeman. The upper floor was sub-let to the Harrisons, a family consisting of husband, wife, and eighteen-month-old baby. They had been tenants for five years and Mrs Harrison was paid a small amount each week to keep an eye on Mrs Davis, who was an invalid.

The late Mrs Davis had suffered from violent epileptic fits for the last twenty-nine years of her life, and from badly ulcerated legs which made movement about the house difficult for her. Although she had been friendly with Mrs Harrison when she first became a tenant, the relationship had soured over the years, generated by Mrs Davis's jealousy of her husband's liking the company of Mrs Harrison – though this friendship appears to have been perfectly innocent.

When Mrs Davis was at last taken to hospital Mrs Harrison visited her there and said that her visit pleased the old lady. Presumably this ended the six weeks of silence from Mrs Davis that she had endured before the latter was taken off to hospital. Mrs Davis did not survive long in hospital but died there on 12 September and was buried at Manor Park Cemetery. The subsequent happenings were described in the *Evening Standard* for 4 February 1938 – the first of many accounts of the disturbances at 132 Teesdale Street:

POLICE AT HOME OF "GHOST" by Garry Allighan

I spent last night in a haunted house in London, investigating the manifestations of a 'ghost' which the BBC are to try to broadcast and televise.

Ghostly manifestations actually occurred while I was there – and were heard by a large crowd gathered in the street.

The fame of the haunted house has spread far and wide, and so great are the crowds attracted that three policemen have been on duty to keep the road clear.

The house is in Bethnal Green. The lower part of it is tenanted by Mr George Davis, a 61-year-old compositor.

'My wife died on September 12th,' Mr Davis told me when I arrived.

Furniture Upset

'On Armistice Day I visited the cemetery with my daughter Grace and my son Sidney. When we returned we heard a strange tapping noise.'

'Like a Morse code signal,' said Sidney, who is 16.

'The noise was repeated at varying intervals during the day, and continued for about two weeks.

'Then, one day, we were having tea in the kitchen when we heard a long-drawn-out moan, followed by heavy footsteps overhead. We rushed up.

'The very heavy tallboy in my father's bedroom which usually stands against the wall, had been moved in the centre of the room. The bedclothes were thrown on the floor. A chair had been overturned.'

Since then the family have not had a minute's peace. Grace Davis, a girl of twenty, told me that the furniture is disturbed about three or four times a day and often during the night.

'It is useless making the beds until the evening,' she said.

'On one occasion the bedroom door was unlocked and a chair was thrown down the stairs.

Picture Turned Over

At another time Grace was standing in the hall talking to Mrs Harrison, who occupies the upper part of the house, and another person.

Suddenly they saw one of the pictures on the wall begin to twist and turn round.

'As I moved forward to steady the picture it was snatched from my hand and dashed to the floor with a crash,' Mrs Harrison told me.

Often when Grace comes down in the morning she finds all the crockery cleared from the kitchen dresser and standing on the table. So far no crockery has been smashed.

Mrs Harrison has had trinkets removed from her dressing-table and placed on the floor.

I had been talking to Mr Davis for about five minutes, when suddenly there was an eerie cry, like that of a woman in pain. I heard heavy footsteps overhead, followed by a loud crash.

We all ran up the stairs, and when we reached the bedroom the door, which Mr Davis swore he had bolted only 15 minutes previously, was standing wide open.

Furniture was overthrown, bedclothes were on the floor.

Mr Davis told me that he had covered a sheet of paper with treacle and placed it on the floor, but although footsteps were heard and furniture was overturned, *there were no marks on the treacle.*

'Last Saturday I tied a chair to the rail of my bed,' he said. 'Three times the string was untied and the chair was overturned. On the

The upturned bedroom chair. (SOCIETY FOR PSYCHICAL RESEARCH)

fourth occasion the chair was overturned and the string disappeared. We called in the police, and they searched every nook and cranny, but the piece of string has not been seen since.'

The family are overwrought and in despair.

It was this report that must have excited the interest of Dr Fodor, the eminent investigator of the International Institute for Psychical Investigation. All but the first of his reports survive in the files of the present-day Society for Psychical Research to whom they were passed when the Institute became defunct. I am most grateful to the Society for allowing me to use them for this account.

Dr Fodor first visited the house on 6 February, accompanied by two assistants, Mr Laurence Evans and the Marquis des Barres.

'We were received with a story of great wonders,' wrote Dr Fodor. Apart from one bang at four in the morning, which had awoken Mr Davis, the night had passed relatively quietly for the occupants of the house, but when Mrs Harrison came downstairs at eight o'clock she found chaos. In the sitting-room, crowded with ornaments, few items were left in their proper place. Pictures of Mrs Davis were upside-down in an armchair when they should have been on the piano; the heavy glass bowl which protected an ornamental pincushion had been removed and the pincushion itself was on the sofa. The cover was also off the birdcage and two chairs were overturned. Furniture was disturbed in other parts of the house too, notably in Grace's bedroom where all the chairs were upside-down and a heavy wardrobe had been moved away from the wall. The family had left everything for the investigators to see.

During the day, Dr Fodor was told, the cry had been heard six times. Mrs Rose, the married daughter, said that it was just like the cry given by her mother before she went into a fit. It was also heard by Mr Abrahams who lived across the street, the newsagent Mr Atkins, and the milkman who had called at eleven o'clock. Usually the cry was followed by a bang and many people smelt a strong and unpleasant odour subsequently which lasted for about five minutes after the bang. The family explained this by associating the bang or thud with Mrs Davis falling at the start of her fit. She would clutch at anything in her distress and often pull it over with her. She would be unconscious for about half an hour and would signal her gradual return to sensibility by a mumbling sound which, it was said, was also frequently heard.

Gradually the investigators were able to discover significant points and learn something of the characters of the people occupying the house. They found the strongest personality to be Mrs Harrison who was inclined to embroider a story given the least encouragement. She exerted considerable influence over the young and timid Gracie with the power of her will. Her husband had little patience with the investigation and when questioned in detail was hostile and evasive. By contrast Mr Davis appeared under-assertive, almost pathetic. After the Harrisons had given Dr Fodor an explicit account of meeting the misty, ethereal form of Mrs Davis on the stairs, Mr Davis was asked whether he had also seen the ghost of his wife. He replied, 'I think she should naturally come to me.'

One of the most significant factors discovered by the investigators was that for the most part the disturbances occurred when the Harrisons were on the top floor. In this report their suspicions about the source of the disturbances fall squarely on the Harrisons:

As to the chair which Mr Davis tied with a string to his bedstead, the string was half a yard long and it was knotted. It was found undone and the chair overturned three times. The string was always lying straight and without knots on the floor. The fourth time Mrs Harrison tied it with a double knot. The chair was overthrown again but the string was gone.

(It seems as if Mr and Mrs Harrison wanted to put an end to an unnecessary complication which required more time to be spent in the bedroom of Mr Davis and was, therefore, more risky. The simplest way out was to take the string.)

They are also sceptical about the picture-turning incident mentioned in the *Evening Standard*, perhaps implying that the picture could have been jerked from the wall by means of a piece of thread held by Mrs Harrison (the classic *modus operandi* of many fake ghosts, including the famous Stockwell Ghost).

The picture was a group photograph on the wall in the passage. It was found turned to the wall. In the presence of Mrs Harrison, Grace turned it round. It seemed to be pulled out of her hand, the nail came out, the picture fell down, and the glass broke.

Finally, they decide that the cry is that of the Harrisons' baby, Maureen, who had made a similar sound earlier during their visit. Her parents maintained that she had only been making that

particular noise for a fortnight or so.

The behaviour of Mr Harrison at the end of their visit had a bizarre touch to it that makes the account border on the hilarious:

> We tried an experiment. We asked Mrs Harrison to lie on Grace's bed and put out the light. The bed did not move, but first three, and later four or five soft taps were heard. It was, however, not impossible for Mrs Harrison to cause them by tapping on the wall. As we went down Mr Evans stayed behind. He heard a noise. Something was thrown down the stairs. It was an onion. He called me back and we called up to Mr Harrison. After some delay he answered. Mr Evans asked him "Was he outside his room just now?" He hesitated and then muttered the baby had thrown down an onion. It was an unusual time for an eighteen-month-old baby to be out in a dark passage throwing onions.

The same investigators visited the house again on the following evening. Their report, remaining sceptical, nevertheless betrays a slight bewilderment with the case; as they get to know the participants better they find it harder to understand why anyone should want to contrive a haunting to frighten the occupants of the house especially since the Harrisons had already expressed their wish to leave it as soon as alternative accommodation could be found. They, like the Davis family, told Dr Fodor of their belief that the disturbances were being caused by the jealous spirit of Mrs Davis trying to force Mrs Harrison from the house.

By questioning the two women separately Fodor was able to show that when two policemen called earlier in the afternoon (Mr Rose was a policeman) and the cry was heard (followed by the throwing down of a chair upstairs) Mrs Harrison had run up to her flat to tend the baby, which was crying. Grace, questioned earlier, had been adamant that all the occupants of the house were present when the policemen called and the cry was heard. The policemen hearing the cry added substantially to the notoriety of the haunting.*

Concluding this report the investigator wrote:

> Mrs Harrison told me that in early November and December, when the cry was new, she used to stand with Grace outside in the rain and cold. They were afraid of the cry and of the opening doors.
> 'The first night we heard the cry,' Mrs Harrison stated, 'Mr

---

*Though this is again contradicted in a later, fifth, report when the policeman, interviewed for a second time, swears that everyone *was* downstairs when the cry was heard.

Harrison was reading and I was knitting. He said "Quick, Mrs Davis". I said, "Don't say that. It is funny, it is her cry". I thought it was Sydney playing a joke on us. I found Sydney below at the door biting his nails. He asked me "Did you hear my Mam?"'

I asked Grace whether anything has been found overthrown in any of the rooms without the door being opened. She said 'Yes'. We then decided to seal up Grace's bedroom on Tuesday afternoon (*the next day*) and leave it sealed up until Thursday afternoon.

Fodor's point about the lack of motive for a phoney haunting was echoed the next day in a statement made by Walter Davis (the unemployed son) to the *Hackney Gazette*. 'People have accused us of telling lies about these things, but it's all perfectly true. What point would there be in making our lives unbearable with crowds packing outside the house and children tormenting us and breaking windows?'

Strangely, no mention of the following strange occurrence is given in the notes of the psychic investigators. Again Walter told the story:

'We hear these cries at all times of the day and night, and they are just the cries my mother used to make when she was ill. Shortly before you arrived we had a visit from a gentleman interested in psychic research. He told us he could see a woman standing in the corner of the room. He described her to us, and the description was exactly that of my mother when she was alive.'

Typically, Mrs Harrison cannot refrain from chipping in:

There was no doubt at all about the description. It was Mrs Davis all right. He also said that she wanted to tell us that she was turning the house up to show us that it was hers, but that we would not have much more of it.

That night must have been a restless one for the Harrisons and the Davis family, but this was due not to the attentions of the ghost but to the crowds which had been drawn to the scene by the publicity. The headline in the *Daily Express* the next morning told of the popular excitement:

'HAUNTED' HOUSE BESIEGED BY 2,000 'GHOST' HUNTERS
DEAD WIFE'S 'I SHALL COME BACK'

Police had to be called last night to control 2,000 determined 'ghost hunters' who were besieging a Bethnal Green house reported to be haunted.

The house is in Teesdale Street, and police had to draw cordons across each end of the road to keep away curious, incredulous sightseers. . . .

Dr Nandor Fodor, research officer of the International Institute for Psychical Research, has been called in by the families, and last night, with two assistants, he took photographs in the house with a special camera. . . . While Dr Fodor was hunting with his camera last night feelings were running high in Teesdale Street.

One woman in the crowd shouted: 'We can't even get into our own street now without having to ask a copper'.

When Laurence Evans came to the house at three in the afternoon he found the occupants still seething with indignation at this report. 'Mrs Harrison was in a high state of hysterics over the *Daily Express* story of the morning,' he wrote. 'She decleared she would not be able to go out of the house owing to the hostility of the women outside.'

Although the night had been peaceful, more disturbances had occurred in the house during the day. After showing the house to Harry Price (a famous psychic investigator later to become notorious for his dubious research at Borley Rectory) Evans began his work of sealing off the front bedroom:

> . . . I then went upstairs into the front room and securely fastened both the windows with 2-inch steel screws, so that neither the top or the bottom could be moved. The Marquis des Barres was helping me, and together we marked the position of every piece of furniture in the room by marking the floor in blue pencil exactly under the leg of each piece. I then sprinkled about two pounds of powdered starch on the floor in the vicinity of the door. We took particular care to make no mark on the floor with our own feet, by sprinkling the floor in front of us and backing out of the room. We then shut the door and I took the following precautions to prevent entry. I had obtained six one-inch steel screw-eyes which I placed in pairs, on the door, one on the lintel in three different places. I then fastened each pair together with 7–22 copper wire. After that I threaded tape through each pair of eyes, wound it round the wire, tied it, and sealed it with my own private seal. I am quite satisfied that it is impossible for normal entry to be made without it being quite apparent to us.

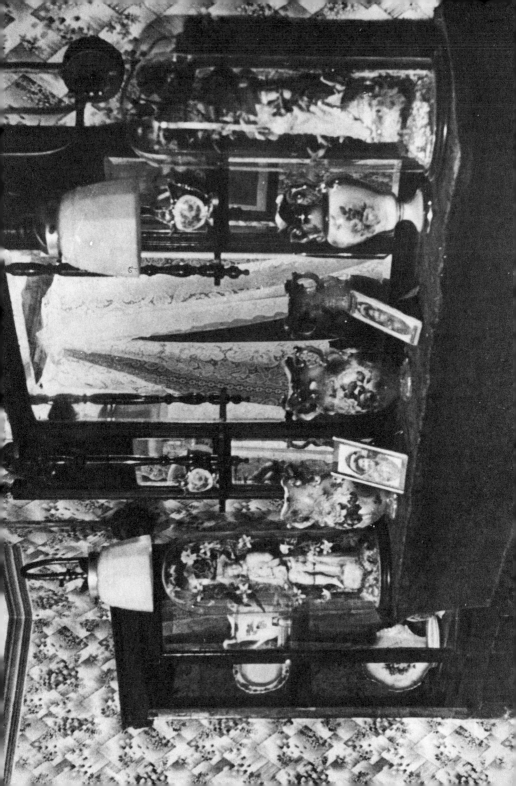

As I was coming down the stairs, preparatory to leaving the house, I heard the moan. It appeared to come from below where Grace, Mrs Harrison and the baby were sitting in the kitchen. I asked them if they had heard it also, and they said that they had and that it had come from the front-room. I went into the front-room and found the glass cover had been taken completely off the near pin-cushion and had been placed on the piano beside it, and the glass cover had been slightly moved from the second pin-cushion.

We left the house at 5 p.m.

On emerging from the house, Evans made the following comments to the reporter from the *Hackney Gazette*:

'So far our investigation has been hampered by a number of things, not the least of which is the presence of large and noisy crowds outside the house. During my stay here this afternoon I have heard the "cry", but I was unable to satisfy myself where it came from.

'I also found that a glass bowl in the sitting room had moved from one part of the room to another, but, as there were fingerprints, this was not very conclusive. However, I have now rubbed all the fingerprints off, and if the bowl moves again the test will be more reliable.

The families in the house have given us the fullest assistance in making our investigation, and in my experience of these matters there would so far appear to be good grounds for believing that something sub-normal is taking place, and that these events are genuine.'

The next visit to the house was made on the Thursday (10 February) to open the room sealed by Laurence Evans two days before. Firstly, however, Dr Fodor investigated articles that had been moved in the front room.

We were told that half-an-hour after Mr Evans left on Tuesday afternoon, the pin-cushion in the sitting room went from under the glass cover on the piano to the sofa. Mr Evans had wiped the glass cover clean before he left. Now, on the glass shade which was moved from the piano to the top of the table we found fingerprints. It would have been an impracticable suggestion to ask the members of the household for fingerprints. Any one of them might have touched the glass shade and forgotten all about it.

It seems today that Fodor was hasty in finding it impracticable to take the fingerprints of everybody in the house. After all the results need not have been revealed, but a closer watch could have been kept on one person in particular.

Another curiosity, in view of the harassment that both families were suffering, is why they stayed in the house at all during this time. Apparently it was suggested that they should all move out and leave it to the investigators for a few days, but this course of action, which seems to be obvious in retrospect, was rejected by all concerned.*

Although the opening of the room proved to be an anti-climax (no furniture had been moved, the starch dust showed no footprints) the usual highly charged atmosphere of the house was quickly re-established with Grace once more in hysterics:

While Mr Evans and myself were talking to the reporters in the sitting-room below, the *Daily Sketch* reporter saw through the glass door of the sitting room Grace showing signs of great agitation and uttering a scream. At that moment the door opened and we were told that they had heard the scream. It seemed to come from above. Mr Evans felt Grace's pulse. Her heart was beating wildly and she was almost crying. Mrs Harrison, at the time the scream was heard, was out in the backyard.

Mr Walter Davis (*the elder son*) heard the scream quite plainly. He said he went cold just before, and expected to hear it.

After the reporters left, Grace went upstairs to sweep up the starch powder. I was with her for some time, then a policeman (No. H 620) who had called, stayed with her while she was doing this work. Below I was questioning Mr Walter Davis whom I met for the first time. He told me about three weeks ago he saw one portrait of Mrs Davis, which was on the mantelpiece in the sitting room, slowly turning around and facing the other. This happened in full light. A number of people have seen it at the same time, including Mrs Harrison and Grace. I asked Mr Walter Davis about the hand which Grace saw coming around the door, and which she recognised as her mother's hand. He said: 'The kitchen door slowly moved. There appeared to be a white shadow behind it, trying to get a grip on the door. I saw no wrist or fingers. I do not know whose hand it might have been.'

Later that day Mrs Pierce, a neighbour, confirmed Walter's tale of the picture turning:

I think it is very mysterious. I have known these people for 33 years. I was there when the picture turned on the mantel-piece to face the other way. Walter and his brother-in-law were there. Mr Harrison was in the kitchen. Ten or fifteen people saw it.

At this time the Vicar, the Reverend F. G. S. Nicholle, was also paying a visit to the house. He had been a witness to strange disturbances there the previous evening when he heard the cry and found a chair thrown across the doorway of the back bedroom. While Fodor was being interviewed by a reporter in the front sitting-room, Sydney, the youngest son, rushed into the room in great excitement and asked them whether they had heard anything. Neither of the men had heard any unusual sounds but both followed Sydney back to the kitchen. Fodor's account continues:

In the kitchen the Vicar told me that tapping noises were heard from above. I went upstairs and found both doors open; the chair in the back bedroom was overthrown. The bolt of that door was drawn. The bolt of the other door was not drawn but this bolt is really not held by the bolt-hole, which is broken through. A little pressure would be sufficient to open it. Such pressure, however, would make a definite noise. I rushed downstairs and asked the Vicar: 'Was everybody in the kitchen whilst this happened?' The Vicar was positive that Mrs Harrison, Mr Walter Davis, Sydney, and Grace were all in the kitchen and no-one had gone upstairs at all.

Mr Evans, while this happened, was outside in the street at the telephone. When he came back he fastened the front door of the sitting-room with copper wire drawn through staples, and placed a large plant-pot at the bottom of the door. He then turned the key in the lock leaving the key inside. Then we turned both pictures of Mrs Davis on the mantel-piece backwards, put one of the pincushions with its cover in the kitchen, and fastened the door between the kitchen and the sitting-room with copper wire drawn through two staples and sealed it. Then we proceeded to the room upstairs and placed the pincushion and its glass cover on the top of Grace's dresser. On the mantel-piece opposite there was a picture of Mrs Davis. This I had turned backwards previous to the door-opening phenomenon. It was still backwards, and so we left it. We fastened the door with copper wire drawn through the top staples and sealed it.

By this time the media had enthusiastically adoped the 'Bethnal Green Ghost' and each day there were reports of the latest developments in the newspaper and on the wireless, as radio was called then. Even that new prodigy television was involved, it being suggested that there should be a transmission from the house. In the Press pundits were being called upon to give their expert interpretations of events, and in the *Evening Standard* of 10 February the authoress Miss Rachael Ferguson commented:

On the evidence, it seems to me that, in view of the fact that the disturbances did not begin until after the burial of Mrs Davis, the trouble comes under the category of 'spirit of the dead', and is, in point of fact, her effort to re-establish communication with her family.

May I suggest, therefore, that Mr Davis and his family should pay serious attention to these 'rappings'?

The method is very simple and is that adopted in table-turning. If these rappings should be heard again, Mr Davis, and his family, should assemble in the room in which the sounds appear to be the clearest and ask, 'Is there anyone there?' If the answer is a rap, he should say, 'We want to help you, and will ask you questions. Rap once for "yes" and twice for "no".'

If this fails, after a thorough test, it has often been found a complete solution to call in a priest to exorcise the house. I say 'often' not 'always' because some spirits are too low in the superphysical scale to be susceptible to prayer.

In this class come poltergeists and elementals, about which there is nothing to be done except to give up the house altogether.

This upsetting of furniture rather points to the poltergeist, but it also possibly indicates the annoyance of the dead at the obtuseness of her family. She probably has something on her mind – remorse, advice, warning, or help – to convey, and should be given every possible help by the living.

The great fame of the haunting brought forward many suggestions of ways of ending the disturbances, both from ordinary members of the public and from the usual cranks. Many suggested exorcism but this remedy was never tried. Contact with a medium was tried at the end of the affair, though since the medium concerned already knew members of the family her pronouncements were too easy to discredit. She failed to disclose anything not already known to the

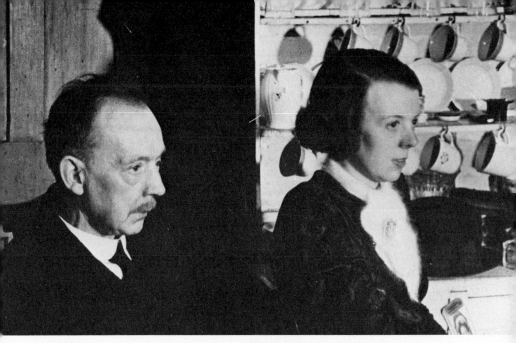

Mr Walter Davis and Grace. (SOC. FOR PSYCHICAL RESEARCH)

family, and Dr Fodor's correspondence with her shows him to have his tongue very much in his cheek.

The report in the *Daily Express* on Friday, 11 February, was also sceptical – pointing out that a ghost able to leave fingerprints was certainly worth investigating. That afternoon the three investigators again visited the house. They asked Grace whether she could see anything strange in the sitting-room through the glass panel of the locked door from the kitchen. She said that she had clearly seen the pictures of Mrs Davis, that Fodor had turned to face the wall, turned back to face the room: then they had turned themselves back to the original position. Mrs Harrison confirmed this, and, indeed, the pictures now faced the wall just as the investigators had left them. Young Sydney Davis was also asked whether he had seen this incident but replied that he was too scared to look for fear of what he might see. In his report Fodor commented:

This statement of the ladies is very odd and throws considerable light on the power of their imagination. I have no doubt whatsoever in my mind that they only imagined the pictures facing them. It would be extremely capricious behaviour on the part of the ghost if in the sealed room it suddenly performed this curious feat.

119

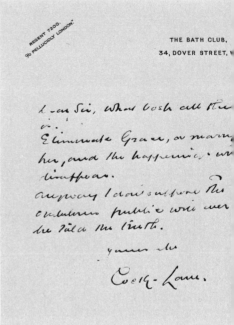

Left: *Another view of the front room.* Right: *The researchers received this amusing letter from the Bath Club.* (SOCIETY FOR PSYCHICAL RESEARCH)

Again, on the Saturday, Dr Fodor and his two assistants visited the house. Newspapermen were maintaining a vigil even though the ghost had scarcely been heard for twenty-four hours, though while they were talking to Grace in the sitting-room she claimed to hear faint moans coming from the kitchen. No one else present heard them. Nothing had been disturbed in either of the sealed rooms. Dr Fodor concluded:

> It is my impression that it has given a shock to the family that the Ghost could not, or would not, manifest in a sealed room. . . . It is as if this shock had set up a doubt in their minds regarding these phenomena, and by this very fact deprived the ghostly agency of one of the principal elements in the psychic atmosphere which made the disturbances possible.

The *Sunday Dispatch* of 13 February carried the story that the Harrisons were to leave the house on the following Tuesday. 'They say they are unable to bear the worry any longer.' The next day in the *Evening Standard* Dr Fodor was forecasting that the disturbances would end within the week. 'I do believe', he is quoted as saying, 'that

120

something very strange is abroad in the house. It is, in fact, one of the strangest cases I have ever met.' He concluded by stressing the difficulties a practical joker would have had playing his tricks in a house so crowded with family, newsmen, police and investigators. Many newspapers writing of the affair noted that poltergeist activity is a haunting of *people* and that in theory the events could continue away from the house. In most cases, they admitted, once a person is persuaded to go by a poltergeist the disturbances cease. As a columnist wrote in the *Daily Mail* on Monday, 14 February:

If we believe in the possibility of poltergeists we shall attribute to them all manner of low cunning and nasty intentions. We cannot be tolerant of them or of their mean, underhand ways. They are altogether different from the honest, upright ghosts of decaying castles and ancient halls. These are respectable ghosts; some are even amiable. Not so poltergeists: they are beyond the pale of this world and the other.

The *North London Recorder* contained a piece on poltergeists by a local occult expert, J. Bardell Smith, suggesting a means of ending the disturbances:

In all poltergeist cases it has been found that there lives in the house a woman in dawning womanhood say from 16 to 21 years of age; and through some mysterious make-up of her physical body 'power' or energy can be drawn by the 'ghost' to move articles, make noises and other very unpleasant demonstrations.

How can these happenings be stopped? The most drastic and certain remedy is the removal of the 'power station' – if the lady of 16 to 21 leaves the house these ghostly demonstrations will certainly come to an end.

In fact this course of action was about to be taken, for the Davis family, like the Harrisons, had also had enough and were looking for accommodation elsewhere. They were increasingly reluctant to speak with the Press or even Dr Fodor. The last mention of the haunting comes in the *City and East London Observer* whose 'Special Representative' accompanied the Doctor when he paid his final visit to the house on 18 February.

Upon our arrival, we were met by Mrs Harrison, the tenant who was moving out that day, and conducted into the kitchen where

Grace Davis, her two brothers and sister-in-law were sitting.

The first question the Doctor asked was 'Has anything happened since I was here last?' The reply came from Grace Davis: 'Owing to the publicity we have received I prefer not to say anything about it.'

After a while, however, Grace and Mrs Harrison told us the following story.

'Last Sunday afternoon we were sitting in this room when Mrs Harrison happened to glance through the communicating door of our front room and saw the outline of a man standing in front of the piano, gazing at an object.'

'She called me and I saw it too,' said Grace. 'Mrs Harrison asked my father to move from the position he was standing in. He did so and the vision still remained. We noticed that my father was in his shirt sleeves, whereas the apparition had a black coat on and a moustache, while my father is clean shaven. This occurred in broad daylight.'

Mrs Harrison here took up the conversation and described once again the sensations she experienced on Friday, when Dr Fodor's assistant and myself persuaded her to lie down on the bed of the late Mrs Davis. She then complained of feeling 'deathly cold', and said she felt as if the back of her head were being pressed in. She seemed to be in a state of coma and clutched her throat, declaring her mouth and throat were dry and sore.

By careful questioning I discovered that Mrs Harrison was the first to see or hear any untoward happening three months ago. She said, 'I saw the figure of Mrs Davis clearly and the word "Go" was uttered distinctly. Immediately after this I visited a London spiritualist who warned me that unless I moved something serious might happen on the middle floor.'

A fear has been on the household for some time due to the disappearance of a piece of string from the bedroom of the late Mrs Davis when a chair was tied to the bed and the 'ghost' decided, after several times untying it, to remove it completely. Every member of the household definitely states that this piece of string was not removed by themselves, and they have spent many hours looking for it, owing to fear of strangulation.

Mrs Harrison, continuing her conversation, stated that she had not told anybody of the fact that she had been to the spiritualist.

Dr Fodor and myself visited the rooms which, it was suggested, had been disturbed since our last visit and could find no traces of upheaval. A quick test by the Doctor showed no results.

He has decided that imagination is playing a part in the later happenings and discounts the theory that the 'ghost' is still present in the house.

As far as the new 'vision' is concerned, we discovered that when the house was being built, a man* was supposed to have fallen off the scaffolding and was killed. Dr Fodor suggested to me that the tenants knowing this, it reacted on their agitated minds, which readily associated the 'vision' with this past occurrence.

To demonstrate his theory, he showed me that a person passing or standing outside the house, their shadow would be thrown and reflected through the front window, and owing to the number of glass objects in the room, could possibly be seen in outline.

Mrs Harrison leaves the house today (Thursday) and Dr Fodor is convinced that the manifestations will not recur.

'I believe in the first place there was a genuine phenomenon behind it,' said Dr Fodor, summing up his conclusions. 'I refuse to believe all that has happened in the house could be due to imagination alone, neither could it have been a hoax. Many things could be explained but others were inexplicable.

'The later happenings are, in my opinion, an aftermath of the original manifestations, due to overwrought nerves. It is the well known last phase of all ghostly disturbances.'

Dr Fodor's notes show that this was not quite the end of the affair. When he contacted the spiritualist she told him that Mrs Harrison had first visited her twelve months previously – well before the death of Mrs Davis. She had been told then to move, 'before there is trouble'. Six weeks before Christmas (after the old lady had died) she again saw Mrs Harrison, this time accompanied by Grace Davis. She was asked to 'psychometrise' Mrs Davis's wedding-ring. Again the message was that Mrs Harrison should go. A few days later the medium came to the house and sat in the chair that Mrs Davis used. This time the warning was even stronger: Mrs Harrison was suspected of helping herself to money while Mrs Davis was in a fit (Mrs Harrison had said earlier that her landlady would often set fire to pound notes when in such a condition). Finally the spiritualist saw the ceiling falling on top of her, which charitably she put down to the condition of the house.

*This was, in fact, Mrs Davis's father, a master builder, who fell to his death while repairing the roof.

There is no escape from the hostility that Mrs Davis felt for Mrs Harrison. The Vicar, the Reverend Francis Nicholle, wrote of it in a letter to Dr Fodor:

I could not discover that Mrs Davis had missed any money after her fits, but she did lose several pieces of jewellery about which I gather she had her suspicions. Mrs Harrison was in the habit of running into debt, and of borrowing money and household things, which was a source of annoyance to Mrs Davis. I understand that she is in Mr Davis' debt, and that is why they have not got rid of her before now.

Mrs Davis evidently disliked her excessively, and kept saying that there would be no peace in the house while she was in it. . . . There can, I think, be no doubt that Mrs H. is the cause of these disturbances, and that their purpose has been either one of hostility, or perhaps of concern for the peace of the family.

Many of the local people thought that the disturbances were caused by the Harrisons, their motive being to escape repaying the money they owed to the Davis family. However there was evidence that the noises, etc. continued even when Mrs Harrison was with reliable witnesses, who claimed that the upper floors were completely empty (presumably Mr Harrison was known to be out at work on these occasions). A daughter of Mrs Davis has written to the author asserting that there was no ill-feeling between the two families, yet dislike and distrust are the emotions that are evoked by the old reports, letters and cuttings. Even Grace, who appears an inseparable companion of the upstairs tenant, expressed her dislike of Mrs Harrison to the Vicar.

Thus the strange story ends, full of contradictions to the last. Nevertheless it would seem that at the heart of the matter there was a genuine supernatural occurrence. Modern stories of poltergeists, such as the one at Enfield described by Guy Playfair, have many facets in common with the happenings at Teesdale Street. More remarkable are the similarities with the Cock Lane Ghost which so disturbed the gentry of London in the eighteenth century. Although part of Teesdale Street survives, the site of the Davis' home (where the family continued to live until the house was demolished in 1956) is now occupied by a great block of council housing, and few people remember the scenes in 1938 when upwards of 2000 people would congregate here in the hope of seeing the ghost.

Crowds outside 132 Teesdale Street. (SOCIETY FOR PSYCHICAL RESEARCH)

Dreams and Omens

The story of Dick Whittington 'turning again' to find fortune in the City of London and become its Lord Mayor three times over is probably the most famous tale of an omen concerning London. The dream of the Swaffham Tinker is hardly less remarkable and has also passed into the folklore of the City. This is how it is told in *Glimpses of the Supernatural* by the Reverend F. G. Lee (1875):

This Tinker, a hard-working, industrious man, one night dreamed that if he took a journey to London, and placed himself at a certain spot on London Bridge, he should meet one who would tell him something of great importance to his future prospects. The Tinker, on whom the dream made a deep impression, related it fully to his wife in the morning; who, however, half-laughed at him and half-scolded him for his folly in heeding such idle fancies. Next night he is said to have redreamed the dream; and again on the third night, when the impression was so powerful on his mind that he determined, in spite of the remonstrances of his wife and the ridicule of his neighbours, to go to London and see the upshot of it. Accordingly he set off for the metropolis on foot, reached it late on the third day (the distance was ninety miles), and, after the refreshment of a night's rest, took his station next day on a part of the Bridge answering to the description in his dream. There he stood all day, and all the next, and all the third, without any communication as to the purpose of his journey; so that towards night, on the third day, he began to lose patience and confidence in his dream, inwardly cursed his folly in disregarding his wife's counsel, and resolved next day to make the best of his way home. He still kept his station, however, till late in the evening, when, just as he was about to depart, a stranger who had noticed him standing steadfastly and with anxious look on the same spot for some days, accosted him, and asked him what he waited there for. After a little hesitation, the Tinker told his errand, though without acquainting him with the name of the place whence he came. The stranger enjoyed a smile at the rustic's simplicity, and advised him to go home and for the future to pay no attention to dreams. 'I myself,' said he, 'if I were disposed to put faith in such things, might now go a hundred miles into the country upon a similar errand. I

Left top: Old London Bridge. (GUILDHALL LIBRARY)
Left: The Swaffham Tinker on a stall-end in the church at Swaffham

dreamed three nights this week that if I went to a place called Swaffham in Norfolk, and dug under an apple-tree in a certain garden on the north side of the town I should find a box of money; but I have something else to do than run after such idle fancies! No, no, my friend; go home, and work well at your calling, and you will find there the riches you are seeking here.' The astonished Tinker did not doubt that this was the communication he had been sent to London to receive, but he merely thanked the stranger for his advice, and went away avowing his intention to follow it. Next day he set out for home, and on his arrival there said little to his wife touching his journey; but next morning he rose betimes and began to dig on the spot he supposed to be pointed out by the stranger. When he had got a few feet down, the spade struck upon something hard, which turned out to be an iron chest. This he quickly carried to his house, and when he had with difficulty wrenched open the lid, found it, to his great joy, to be full of money. After securing his treasure, he observed on the lid of the box an inscription, which, unlearned as he was, he could not decipher. But by a stratagem he got the description read without any suspicion on the part of his neighbours by some of the Grammar School lads, and found it to be

'Where this stood
Is another twice as good.'

And in truth on digging again the lucky Tinker disinterred, below the place where the first chest had lain, a second twice as large, also full of gold and silver coin. It is stated that, become thus a wealthy man, the Tinker showed his thankfulness to Providence by building a new chancel to the church, the old one being out of repair. And whatever fiction the marvellous taste of those ages may have mixed up with the tale, certain it is that there is shown to this day a monument in Swaffham Church, having an effigy in marble, said to be that of the Tinker with his Dog at his side and his tools and implements of trade lying about him.

A remarkable dream led to the arrest of a man for murder in 1695. On 23 December of that year a Grub Street grocer named Stockden was killed and no clue to the identity of the murderer was found. A few days later a Mrs Greenwood visited a local magistrate and told him that Stockden had appeared to her in a dream and begged her to tell the authorities that the man who had killed him lived in a house in Thames Street, which she was able to describe. The following night she had dreamed again, and this time Stockden showed her a portrait of the murderer, saying that his name was Maynard.

The magistrate accordingly sent for Maynard and questioned him about the killing, whereupon he confessed that he had been one of those who had killed the unfortunate grocer, but that he had three accomplices, whose identity he refused to divulge at first. However Mrs Greenwood dreamed yet again, and this time Stockden showed her a portrait of one of the accomplices, and through this identification the man was arrested. The third culprit was then betrayed by Maynard, and all three were hanged for the crime, which had been solved by a dream.

A further example of how a dream, and a ghost, led to justice being done comes from J. H. Ingram's *Haunted Homes and Family Traditions of Great Britain*. (1884). He found the story in *The History and Reality of Apparitions*, published in 1770 and edited by Defoe, who says that its source, the Reverend Dr Scott, was not only a man 'whose learning and piety were eminent, but one whose judgment was known to be good.' This is the story as told in *Haunted Homes*:

Dr. Scott was sitting alone by his fireside in the library of his house in Broad Street; he had shut himself in the room to study and, so it is alleged, had locked the door. In the midst of his reading happening to look up, he was much astounded to see, sitting in an elbow-chair on the other side of the fire-place, a grave, elderly gentleman, in a black velvet gown and a long wig, looking at him with a pleased countenance, and as if about to speak. Knowing that he had locked the door, Dr. Scott was quite confounded at seeing this uninvited visitor sitting in the elbow-chair, and from the first appears to have suspected its supernatural character. Indeed, so disturbed was he at the sight of the apparition, for such it was, that he was unable to speak, as he himself acknowledged in telling the story. The spectre, however, began the discourse by telling the doctor not to be frightened, for it would do him no harm, but came to see him upon a matter of great importance to an injured family, which was in danger of being ruined. Although the doctor was a stranger to this family, the apparition stated that knowing him to be a man of integrity it had selected him to perform an act of great charity as well as justice.

At first Dr. Scott was not sufficiently composed to pay proper attention to what the apparition propounded; but was rather more inclined to escape from the room if he could, and made one or two futile attempts to knock for some of his household to come up; at which his visitor appeared to be somewhat displeased. But, as the doctor afterwards stated, he had no power to go out of the room, even if he had been next the door, nor to knock for help, even if any had been close at hand.

Then the apparition, seeing the doctor still so confused, again desired him to compose himself, assuring him that he would not do him the slightest injury, nor do anything to cause him the least uneasiness, but desired that he would permit him to deliver the business he came about, which, when he had heard, he said, he would probably see less cause to be surprised or apprehensive than he did now.

By this time Dr. Scott had somewhat recovered himself, and encouraged by the calm manner in which the apparition addressed him, contrived to falter out:

'In the name of God, what art thou?'

'I desire you will not be frightened,' responded the apparition. 'I am a stranger to you, and if I tell you my name you will not know it. But you may do the business without inquiring further.' The doctor could not compose himself, but still remained very uneasy, and for some time said nothing. Again the apparition attempted to reassure him, but could only elicit from him a repetition of the ejaculation, 'In the name of God, what art thou?'

Upon this, says the narration, the spectre appeared to be displeased, and expostulated with Dr. Scott, telling him that it could have terrified him into compliance, but that it chose to come quietly and calmly to him; and, indeed, made use of such civil and natural discourse that the doctor began to grow a little more familiar, and at last ventured to ask what it wanted of him. Upon this the apparition appeared to be very gratified, and began its story. It related that it had once owned a very good estate, which at that time was enjoyed by its grandson; two nephews, however, the sons of its younger brother, were then suing for possession of the property and, owing to certain family reasons which the doctor could not or would not specify, were likely to oust the young man from his property. A deed of settlement, being the conveyance of the inheritance, could not be found and without it the owner of the estate had every reason to fear he would be ejected.

'Well,' said Dr. Scott, 'what can I do in the case?'

'Go to my grandson,' said the apparition, 'and direct him where to find the missing deed, which is concealed in a place where I put it myself.' And then it gave the doctor minute particulars of the chest wherein the needed document was hidden stowed away in an old lumber-room. When the apparition had impressed the matter thoroughly upon the doctor's mind, Dr. Scott not unnaturally asked his visitor why it could not direct the grandson himself to recover the missing deed. 'Ask me not about that,' said the apparition; 'there are divers reasons, which you may know hereafter. I can depend upon your honesty in it in the meantime.'

Still Dr. Scott did not like to take upon himself the strange mission, whereupon the apparition seemed to grow angry, and even begin to threaten him, so that he was at last compelled to promise compliance. The apparition then assumed a pleasant aspect, thanked him, and disappeared.

The strangest part of this strange story yet remains to be told. At the earliest opportunity Dr. Scott posted away to the address given him by the apparition, or dream as some persons deemed it. He asked for and was at once introduced to the gentleman the apparition had sent him to, and to his surprise was received most cordially by him. Dr. Scott's surprise was, indeed, quickened when the stranger entered most unreservedly into the particulars of his law-suit, telling him that he had had a dream the previous night, in which he had dreamed that a strange gentleman came to him, and assisted him to find the deed which was needed to confirm him in the possession of his estate.

This assured Dr. Scott that it was not a dream which he had had, and that he was really selected to discover the missing document. Making himself agreeable to his host, he eventually got him to take him all over his splendid old mansion. Finally, he beheld just such a lumber-room as the apparition had told him of, and on entering it, saw an exact *fac-simile* of the chest described to him by his supernatural visitant. There was an old rusty key in it that would neither turn round, nor come out of the lock, which was exactly what the apparition had forwarned him of! At the doctor's request a hammer and chisel were sent for, and the chest broken open, and, after some difficulty, a false drawer was found in it. This being split open, *there lay the missing parchment* spread out flat over the whole breadth of the bottom of the trunk!

The Crypt at Bow Church. (GUILDHALL LIBRARY)

The joy of the young heir, and of his family, may be imagined, whilst their surprise can have been no less. Whether Dr. Scott informed them of the means by which he was led to make the discovery is not stated; but it is alleged the production of the needed deed confirmed the owner in the possession of his estates. As this gentleman was still living, the narrator was not inclined to publish his name; and, now-a-days, the chances of discovering it are, doubtless, far less than they were in his time of finding the missing document. Regard it how we may, as a dream or a coincidence, certainly Dr. Scott's adventure was a very marvellous one.

A more macabre episode is described in a great source of material on dreams, the Reverend F. G. Lee's *Glimpses of the Supernatural*. It shows again how greatly the ghoulish activities of the 'resurrectionists' were feared at that time:

The Rev. Mr. Perring, Vicar of a parish which is now a component part of London, though, about forty-five years ago it had the appearance of a village at the outskirts, had to encounter the sad affliction of losing his eldest Son at an age when parents are encouraged to believe their children are to become their survivors; the youth dying in his seventeenth year. He was buried in the vaults of the church.

Two nights subsequently to that interment, the father dreamed that he saw his Son habited in a shroud spotted with blood, the expression of his countenance being that of a person enduring some paroxysm of acute pain: 'Father, father! come and defend me!' were the words he distinctly heard, as he gazed on this awe-inspiring apparition; 'they will not let me rest quietly in my coffin.'

The venerable man awoke with terror and trembling; but after a brief interval of painful reflection concluded himself to be labouring under the influence of his sad day-thoughts, and the depression of past sufferings; and with these rational assurances commended himself to the All-Merciful, and slumbered again and slept.

He saw his Son again beseeching him to protect his remains from outrage, 'For,' said the apparently surviving dead one, 'they are mangling my body at this moment.' The unhappy Father rose at once, being now unable to banish the fearful image from his mind, and determined when day should dawn to satisfy himself of the delusiveness or verity of the revelation conveyed through this seeming voice from the grave.

At an early hour, accordingly, he repaired to the Clerk's house, where the keys of the church and of the vaults were kept. The Clerk after considerable delay, came down-stairs, saying it was very unfortunate he should want them just on that very day, as his son over the way had taken them to the smith's for repair, – one of the largest of the bunch of keys having been broken off short in the main door of the vault, so as to render it impracticable for anybody to enter till the lock had been picked and taken off.

Impelled by the worst misgivings, the Vicar loudly insisted on the Clerk's accompanying him to the blacksmith's – not for a key but for a crowbar, it being his resolute determination to enter the vault and see his Son's coffin without a moment's delay.

The recollections of the dream were now becoming more and more vivid, and the scrutiny about to be made assumed a solemnity mingled with awe, which the agitation of the father rendered terrible to the agents in this forcible interruption into the resting-place of the dead. But the hinges were speedily wrenched asunder – the bar and bolts were beaten in and bent beneath the heavy hammer of the smith, – and at length with tottering and outstretched hands, the maddened parent stumbled and fell: his son's coffin had been lifted from the recess at the vault's side and deposited on the brick floor; the lid, released from every screw, lay loose at top, and the body, enveloped in its shroud, on which were several dark spots below the chin, lay exposed to view; the head had been raised, the broad riband had been removed from under the jaw, which now hung down with the most ghastly horror of expression, as if to tell with more terrific certainty the truth of the preceding night's vision. *Every tooth in the head had been drawn.*

The young man had when living a beautiful set of sound teeth. The Clerk's Son, who was a barber, cupper, and dentist, had possessed himself of the keys, and eventually of the teeth, for the purpose of profitable employment of so excellent a set in his line of business. The feelings of the Rev. Mr. Perring can be easily conceived. The event affected his mind through the remaining term of his existence; but what became of the delinquent whose sacrilegious hand had thus rifled the tomb was never afterwards correctly ascertained. He decamped the same day, and was supposed to have enlisted as a soldier. The Clerk was ignominiously displaced, and did not long survive the transaction. Some years afterwards, his house was pulled down to afford room for extensive improvements and new buildings in the village.

As regards the occurrence itself, few persons were apprised of it; as the Vicar – shunning public talk and excitement on the subject of any member of his family – exerted himself in concealing the circumstances as much as possible. The above facts, however, may be strictly relied on as accurate.

The most spectacular portents heralded the Plague which struck London in the early summer of 1665. Similar signs were seen a year later, before the Great Fire. This description of the first omens that were seen comes from *The Terrific Register* of 1825:

In the first place, a blazing star or comet appeared for several months before the plague, as there did the year after another, a little before the fire; the old women, and the phlegmatic hypochondriac part of the other sex, who I could almost call old women too, remarked (especially afterwards, though not till these judgments were over,) that those two comets passed directly over the city, and that so very near the houses, that it was plain they imported something peculiar to the city alone; that the comet before the pestilence, was of a faint, dull, languid colour, and its motion very heavy, solemn, and slow: but that the comet before the fire, was bright and sparkling, or as others said, flaming, and its motion swift and furious; and that accordingly, one foretold a heavy judgment, slow but severe, terrible and frightful, as was the plague; but the other foretold a stroke, sudden, swift, and fiery as the conflagration; nay, so particular some people were, that as they looked upon that comet preceding the fire, they fancied that they not only saw it pass swiftly and fiercely, and could perceive the motion with their eye, but even they heard it; that it made a rushing mighty noise, fierce and terrible, though at a distance, and but just perceivable.

Some heard voices warning them to be gone, for that there would be such a plague in London, so that the living would not be able to bury the dead: others saw apparitions in the air. Here they told us, they saw a flaming sword held in a hand, coming out of a cloud, with a point hanging directly over the city. There they saw hearses and coffins in the air, carrying to be buried. And there again, heaps of dead bodies lying unburied, and the like.

Another ran about naked, except a pair of drawers about his waist, crying day and night, like a man that Josephus mentions, who cried, 'Woe to Jerusalem!' a little before the destruction of that city: so this poor naked creature cried, 'Oh! the great and dreadful God!' and said no more, but repeated those words continually, with a voice and countenance full of horror, a swift pace, and nobody could ever find him to stop, or rest, or take any sustenance, at least, that ever I could hear of. I met this poor creature several times in

Solomon Eagle became famous in London during the time of the Plague for his denunciations of the weaknesses of Mankind. He was known as the Enthusiast.
(GUILDHALL LIBRARY)

the streets, and would have spoken to him, but he would not enter into speech with me, or any one else; but held on his dismal cries continually.

In a narrow passage by Bishopsgate church-yard stood a man looking through between the palisadoes into the burying place; and as many people as the narrowness of the passage would admit to stop, without hindering the passage of others; and he was talking mighty eagerly to them, and pointing now to one place, then to another, and affirming, that he saw a ghost walking upon such a grave-stone there; he described the shape, the posture, and the movement of it so exactly, that it was the greatest matter of amazement to him in the world, that every body did not see it as well as he. On a sudden he would cry, 'There it is: now it comes this way:' then ''tis turned back;' till at length he persuaded the people into so firm a belief of it, that one fancied he saw it, and another fancied he saw it; and thus he came every day making a strange hubbub, considering it was in so narrow a passage, till Bishopsgate clock struck eleven; and then the ghost would seem to start; and as if he were called away, disappeared on a sudden.

The most curious portent of the Plague was given not in London but many miles to the west, in Cornwall. The Botathen Ghost is one of the greatest of our native ghost stories, and it needs little excuse to tell it again here.

The ghost first appeared to a schoolboy named Bligh, who encountered it each day as he crossed a field on his way to and from school. It was dressed 'in female attire' and would glide past him three or four times as he walked through the field. He became so upset by the apparition that he began to make a long detour to avoid going through Botathen (the name of the district where the ghost appeared – it is about three miles from Padstow). His family soon noticed a change in his demeanour and eventually got him to tell them what it was that was troubling him. When he told of the ghost they showed a little disbelief, but all the same approached his schoolmaster, the Reverend John Ruddle, a Prebendary of Exeter and Vicar of Alternan, and told him their son's story. When he heard it he was impressed by their sincerity and agreed to accompany the boy on a walk through the haunted meadow. In his diary the clergyman wrote of his first meeting with the ghost:

I arose the next morning, and went with him. The field to which he led me I guessed to be about twenty acres, in an open country, and about three furlongs from any house. We went into the field, and had not gone a third part before the *spectrum*, in the shape of a woman, with all the circumstances that he had described the day before, so far as the suddenness of its appearance and transition would permit me to discover, passed by.

I was a little impressed at it, and, though I had taken up a firm resolution to speak to it, I had not the power, nor durst I look back; yet I took care not to show any fear to my pupil and guide; and therefore, telling him that I was satisfied in the truth of his statement, we walked to the end of the field, and returned: nor did the ghost meet us that time but once.

There follows an account of several subsequent meetings with it. Mr Ruddle was an observant and fearless investigator: he noted that his spaniel was aware of the ghost's presence as it barked at it and then ran away. His description of the way it moved formed the pattern for many later 'ghost-writers':

> . . . secondly the motion of the *spectrum* was not *gradatim* or by steps, or moving of the feet, but by a kind of gliding, as children upon ice, or as a boat down a river, which practically answers the description the ancients give of the motion of these lemures.

By getting local people to accompany him to the field, Ruddle was able to identify the ghost as being Dorothy Durant (Dinglet in another account), a woman of the district who had often visited the Blighs and who had died a short time previously. His attempts to get the ghost to tell him what troubled it were unsuccessful. It answered in a voice that was hardly audible, and even the words he heard were unintelligible. Thus he decided that the only solution was to exorcise it: by these means the ghost could properly divulge the reason for its presence and thus be put to rest. Accordingly Ruddle set off secretly to Exeter to obtain permission from the Bishop. It proved difficult to persuade the latter that such action should be taken as he was reluctant to sanction anything that smacked of Popery.

'Our Church,' he told Ruddle, 'as is well known, hath abjured certain branches of her ancient power, on grounds of perversion and abuse.' But the country schoolmaster had done his homework, and by quoting from the seventy-second Canon of 1604 was able to convince his Bishop that permission should be granted.

Thus Ruddle was able to return to Botathen with the licence for exorcism signed and sealed, though as he knelt before the Bishop to receive his blessing, the old man had whispered: 'Let it be secret, Mr Ruddle, – weak brethren, weak brethren!'

The exorcism itself, as described in Ruddle's diary, seems to come straight from the pages of Denis Wheatley:

January 12th, 1665. Rode into the gateway of Botathen, armed at all points, but not with Saul's armour, and ready. There is danger from the demons, but so there is in the surrounding air every day. At early morning then and alone, for so the usage ordains, I betook me towards the field. It was void, and I had thereby due time to prepare. First I paced and measured out my circle on the grass. Then did I mark my pentacle in the very midst, and at the intersection of the five angles I did set up and fix my crutch of raun [rowan]. Lastly I took my station south, at the true line of the meridian, and stood facing due north. I waited and watched for a long time. At last there was a kind of trouble in the air, a soft and rippling sound, and all at once the shape appeared, and came on towards me gradually. I opened my parchment scroll, and read aloud the command. She paused and seemed to waver and doubt; stood still: and then I rehearsed the sentence again, sounding out every syllable like a chant. She drew near my ring, but halted at first outside, on the brink. I sounded again, and now at the third time I gave the signal in Syriac – the speech which is used, they say, where such ones dwell and converse in thoughts that glide.

She was at last obedient and swam into the midst of the circle: and there stood still suddenly. I saw, moreover, that she drew back her pointing hand. All this while I do confess that my knees shook under me, and the drops of sweat ran down my flesh like rain. But now, although face to face with the spirit, my heart grew calm and my mind composed, to know that the pentacle would govern her, and the ring must bind until I gave the word. Then I called to mind the rule laid down of old that no angel or fiend, no spirit, good or evil, will ever speak until they be spoken to. N.B. – This is the great law of prayer. God Himself will not yield reply until man hath made vocal entreaty once and again. So I went on to demand, as the books advise; and the phantom made answer willingly. Questioned, wherefore not at rest? Unquiet because of a certain sin. Asked what and by whom? Revealed it; but it is *sub sigillo*, and therefore *nefas*

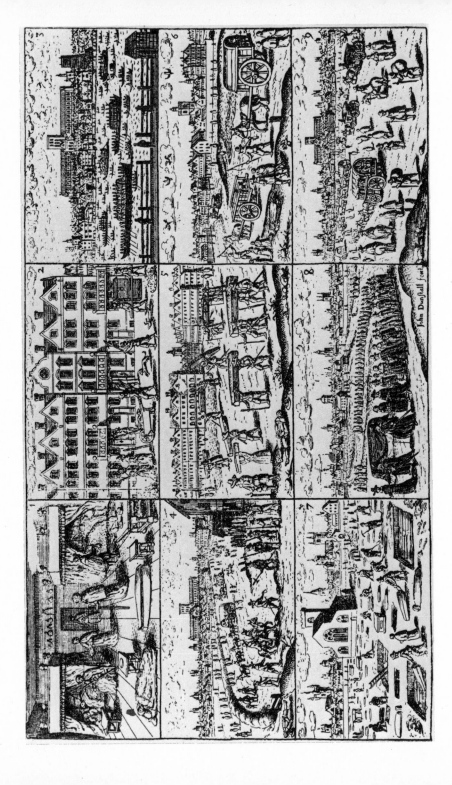

John Dunstall fecit

dictu; more anon. Inquired, what sign she could give me that she was a true spirit and not a false friend? Stated [that] before next Yule-tide a fearful pestilence would lay waste the land; and myriads of souls would be loosened from their flesh, until, as she piteously said, 'Our valleys will be full.' Asked again, why she so terrified the lad? Replied, 'It is the law; we must seek a youth or a maiden of clean life, and under age, to receive messages and admonitions.' We conversed with many more words; but it is not lawful for me to set them down. Pen and ink would degrade and defile the thoughts she uttered, and which my mind received that day. I broke the ring and she passed, but to return once more next day. At evensong a long discourse with that ancient transgressor, Mr. B—. Great horror and remorse; entire atonement and penance; whatsoever I enjoin; full acknowledgment before pardon.

January 13, 1665. At sunrise I was again in the field. She came in at once, and, as it seemed, with freedom. Inquired if she knew my thoughts, and what I was going to relate? Answered, 'Nay, we only know what we perceive and hear: we cannot see the heart.' Then I rehearsed the penitent words of the man she had come up to denounce, and the satisfaction he would perform. Then said she, 'Peace in our midst.' I went through the proper forms of dismissal, and fulfilled all, as it was set down and written in my memoranda; and then with certain fixed rites, I did dismiss that troubled ghost, until she peacefully withdrew, gliding towards the west. Neither did she ever afterwards appear; but was allayed, until she shall come in her second flesh, to the Valley of Armageddon on the Last Day.

Thus ends a wonderful story; only Ruddle's triumph at the advent of the Plague strikes an unhappy note to modern ears. This is the entry in his diary for 10 July 1665:

How sorely must the infidels and hereticks of this generation be dismayed when they know that this Black Death, which is now swallowing its thousands in the streets of the great city was foretold six months agone, under the exorcisms of a country minister, by a visible and suppliant ghost! And what pleasures and improvements do such deny themselves who scorn and avoid all opportunity of intercourse with souls separate, and the spirits, glad and sorrowful, which inhabit the unseen world.

A pictorial broadsheet of 1665 showing the grim scenes during the Plague. (GUILDHALL LIBRARY)

Bibliography

Abbot, G.   *Ghosts of the Tower of London*, 1980
Arminian Magazine, 1781
Aubrey, John   *Anecdotes*
Bailey, James Blake
(*editor*)   *Diary of a Resurrectionist*, 1896
Bovet, Richard   *Pandaemonium*, 1684
Braddock, Joseph   *Haunted Houses*, 1956
Brown, Raymond Lamont *Phantoms of the Sea*
Emslie, J. P.   See *London Studies*, No. 1, 1974
Farson, Daniel   *Hamlyn Book of Ghosts*
Gentleman's Magazine   Various issues
Grant, Douglas   *The Cock Lane Ghost*, 1965
Green, Andrew   *Our Haunted Kingdom*, 1975
Haining, Peter   *The Mystery and Horrible Murders of Sweeney Todd*, 1979
Hallam, J.   *Ghosts of London*, 1975
Harper, Charles   *Haunted Houses*, 1907, 1931
Hopkins, Thurston   *Ghosts over England*
Howitt, W.   *Northern Heights of London*
Hutton, Luke   *The Black Dogge of Newgate*, 1638
Ingram, J. H.   *The Haunted Houses and Family Traditions of Great Britain*, 1884
Jarvis, T. M.   *Accredited Ghost Stories*, 1823
Knapp and Baldwin   *New Newgate Calendar*
Lambert, G. W.   'Geography of London Ghosts', from *Proceedings of the Society for Psychical Research*, No. 720
Lee, F. G.   *Glimpses of the Supernatural*, 1875
   Sights and Shadows, 1894
Linebaugh, P.   *Albion's Fatal Tree*, 1975
Maple, Eric   *The Realm of Ghosts*, 1964
   Supernatural England, 1977
Notes & Queries   Various issues
O'Donnell, Elliot   *Haunted Houses of London*, 1909
   More Haunted Houses of London, 1920
Palmer, Samuel   *History of St Pancras*, 1870
Prickett, E.   *History of Highgate*
Rollins, H. E.   *The Pack of Autolycus*, 1931
Shute, Nerina   *London Villages*, 1973
'Spectre Stricken'   *Ghostly Visitors*, 1882
The Terrific Register, 1825
Underwood, Peter   *Haunted London*, 1973
Walford, E.   *Old and New London*
Welby, H.   *Mysteries of Life*, 1861
   Signs before Death, 1875

Index